front porch PARENTING

*To families and friends
of Mt. Olive Lutheran
Church:*

Mary Mary Simon 6-26-97

front porch
PARENTING

DR. MARY MANZ SIMON

Chariot VICTOR
PUBLISHING
A DIVISION OF COOK COMMUNICATIONS

Victor Books is an imprint of ChariotVictor Publishing
Cook Communications, Colorado Springs, CO 80918
Cook Communications, Paris, Ontario
Kingsway Communications, Eastbourne, England

FRONT PORCH PARENTING
© 1997 by Mary Manz Simon

Cover design by B.C. Studios
Cover illustration by Jeff Stoddard
First printing, 1997
Printed in the United States of America
01 00 99 98 97   5 4 3 2 1

Library of Congress Cataloging-in-Publication Data

Simon, Mary Manz, 1948-
       Front porch parenting : down-to-earth answers to 300 questions real
parents ask / Mary Manz Simon.
              p.   cm.
       Includes index.
       ISBN 0-7814-0306-5
       1. Parenting—United States. 2. Parent and child—United States.
       3. Child rearing—United States. Child development—United
       States. 5. Child psychology—United States. I. Title.
       HQ755.85.S538 1997   96-43349
       649'.1—dc20   CIP

Some material in *Front Porch Parenting* appeared previously in the Belleville,
Illinois *News-Democrat* or *Christian Parenting Today* magazine.

Dedication

For the special people in Toronto who combined their vision and talents to launch the ground-breaking television program, "Just for Parents:" Bruce and Elaine Stacey, Moira and Richard Brown, Paul Kelly, George McEachern, Penny Spence, and Cheryl Weber

Contents

Section One:

Age-Related Questions and Answers

Section Two:

General Questions and Answers

Introduction

"My children are usually good, except when I'm talking on the phone. Help!"

"Can I take my boys with me into the women's rest room?"

"How do I start to teach my child to pray?"

For decades, parents have asked questions similar to these. Today we still ask the questions, but there is one key difference: we have no one to answer them.

We can't sit on the front porch and talk to Aunt Carol; her leisure time is filled with travel and volunteering. We don't know the neighbor, so we can't talk across the backyard fence. And we can't ask Dad, because he's busy starting his third career after retiring.

It shouldn't be difficult to find someone with whom to discuss ordinary questions about everyday parenting. It shouldn't be difficult, but it is.

As a result, today's parents are some of the loneliest people in the world. I know: I've answered their calls for help.

As parenting columnist for both a weekly newspaper and a national magazine, my mailbox is filled with letters.

As a media personality, I've talked with hundreds of callers on live call-in shows.

As a speaker, I've addressed thousands of parents, educators, and grandparents.

I've observed that those of us who care for children don't need flashy ideas; we just need ideas that will work. We need answers to those irritating little problems that don't seem "important" enough to be addressed in reference books. And yet some of our most intense parenting is woven into the fabric of everyday life.

That's why I wrote this book. To answer nagging questions like, "Should I tell my child his IQ?" To give explanations about why a child might still be grieving months after a dog ran away. To affirm the parent who seeks alternatives to candy in the Easter basket. And to encourage you, who nurture a new generation.

This isn't a coffee-table book; this is a real-life-parenting book. Add notes, underline key phrases, or do anything else that makes this your parenting book. Keep it in the car in case basketball practice runs long, or next to the rocking chair for the times you can take an extra moment to hold that sleeping toddler. Use the table of contents if you're browsing; refer to the detailed index for help with specific issues. It's my hope that this single volume will provide answers to questions throughout the years of childhood.

As I type these words today, I feel a sense of connectedness with you. Like you, I have waited anxiously for a child's X-rays in an emergency room and chased round cereal rolling down a church aisle. As my daughter, Angela, once said when introducing me, "Her stage name is Dr. Mary Manz Simon. Her real name is Mom."

So imagine we've just met in the school hallway, and you need a sounding board. Come, walk alongside me, as you and I share some of the joys and challenges of parenting.

Section One

AGE-RELATED

QUESTIONS AND ANSWERS

Chapter One

Infants and Toddlers

BIRTH TO TWO YEARS OLD

- Right child-rearing book
- Cheaper to breast-feed
- Bottle guilt
- Spoil a baby?
- Finding a baby-sitter
- Useful shower gifts
- What's wrong with me?
- Smarter if I read to him?
- Covers on baby
- Diaper changes
- Exhaustion
- Equal attention
- Worry

- Needing sleep
- Teaching prayer
- Baby talk
- Don't enjoy mothering
- Too early for "terrible twos"?
- Still a "terrible two"!
- TV baby-sitter
- Public place survival kit
- Toy box
- Daily bath
- Encourage vs. push
- Day care definitions

Q   *How do I know which parenting book or magazine gives the right answers?*

A   Our parenting is based on values, priorities, and personal style. Refer to an expert with experience and education who appears to be a good match for you.

Often, there is not a single right or wrong answer to parenting questions. There can even be two or three right answers to the same problem!

Whatever source you choose, read the information, then selectively apply that to your situation. Remember, you are still the expert on your child.

🐀 🐀 🐀 🐀 🐀 🐀 🐀

Q   *I love my obstetrician, but how do I find a baby doctor who is just as great as he is?*

A   Obviously, you have talked openly and honestly with your doctor through the pregnancy, trust him, and have a lot of confidence in his abilities. These are the same qualities you will need in your child's doctor.

"Doctor shopping" begins by checking the list of medical personnel eligible for coverage under your health-care plan. Look under two categories: pediatricians and family practitioners. Decide if you want someone who cares just for your child or will care for everyone in your family. Then ask your trusted obstetrician and friends for a list of suggestions.

Also identify special needs. If you have a family history of allergies, look for someone with special training in this area.

As a soon-to-be-mom, I was strongly committed to breast-feeding. I phoned the hospital nursery and asked a nurse, "Which pediatricians are most supportive of nursing moms?" That simple question narrowed down the list of potential pediatricians to three people!

Your list will be smaller after taking each of these steps. Next, phone the office of doctors remaining on the list and ask basic questions:

• When are the office hours? Most health-care professionals offer evening and weekend appointments, but check to be sure.

• Who covers on days off and vacations?

• Which hospitals does the doctor use?

• Whom do patients see on well-baby visits? Some doctors rotate office hours with other physicians or work together with a pediatric nurse practitioner. Find out now so you aren't surprised later.

• In an emergency, how do I contact the doctor?

Once you've narrowed your selection, request a ten-minute appointment with the final candidates. Which competent doctor appears to match your needs? Which seems most willing and able to address your questions and concerns? A personal meeting can quickly help you determine exactly which doctor you'd like to care for your child. So, as you will do in so many issues of parenting, gather all the information possible, then use your best judgment.

Q Is it cheaper to breast-feed?

A Breast-feeding is cheaper than bottle-feeding.

Stores and mail-order companies offer special breast/feeding blouses, bras, extraction pumps, and pads. You can probably get along without any of those things. A nursing bra is handy, especially when you breast*f*feed away from home. A nursing nightgown is convenient but not essential for middle-of-the-night feedings. You won't need a pump if you and your baby will be together all the time. A clean handkerchief will absorb milk drops just as well, or better, than any purchased pad.

What you need to support breast-feeding are things that money can't buy: at least one person (husband, mother, etc.) who will continually encourage and support you, lots of fluids, a helpful pediatrician, and lots of rest.

Many mothers find a lactation consultant invaluable. A lactation consultant will advise you in your first attempts to nurse the baby and offer ongoing help in the months that follow. To locate a lactation consultant in your area, call the International Lactation Consultant Association at 312-541-1710. Also ask your local hospital if they have a breast-feeding hot line. Or look in your phone book for the local branch of the LaLeche League. If possible, attend a breast-feeding information session or a LaLeche meeting before you give birth.

Support, encouragement, and information are three critical aspects to build into your postpartum weeks. Contact with supportive people, especially moms who are currently nursing, is far more important than a nursing gown or breast pump.

Q Breast-feeding my daughter was a struggle, and I'm so glad I quit. I still feel guilty, though, when I see one of my friends nursing her baby.

A Although theoretically any healthy mother/child pair can be a successful nursing couple, in practice, breast-feeding is easier for some than for others. But a breast-fed or bottle-fed baby can be happy and healthy. A nursing or bottle-feeding mom can be a loving, effective parent.

What's important is that your baby's nutritional and health needs are met, that she's talked to, smiled at, and comforted, and that she lives in a safe place with loving people.

You have already made the breast-or-bottle decision. From what you indicated, that choice was best for you and your family at the time. Don't let self-doubt rob you of the growing confidence you could feel as a mom.

You will face many other choices as a parent: training pants or diapers during toilet training, sending to preschool or not, institutional or home day care, self-care or after-school care by an agency, letting your child earn a poor homework grade or doing the work for him, etc. Sometimes you will choose correctly; other times you will make a wrong decision. Many times there won't be a right choice, but simply a judgment.

In all of these situations, do as you did with this decision: parent as well as you can. Observe various styles of parenting, and consider different options, but choose what works best for you and your family.

Q Can you spoil a new baby?

A No. A newborn who whimpers or cries is asking to be changed, fed, soothed, or held. These baby sounds are typically called cuddle communications. Infants (and their parents) need lots of hugs and soothing words.

Q How do I find a baby-sitter who can care for my baby in my
house?

A The best sources for in-home child care are referrals from
friends, neighbors, and family members who use child care.
Also contact local elementary schools. Sometimes moms or
grandparents who care for children during after-school hours are
willing to give all-day child care to an infant. Also ask your child-
birth instructor, pediatrician, or breast-feeding consultant for
referrals.

Whether you use these sources, place an ad in your church
newsletter, or read nanny ads in the phone book, these are just
starting points. Conduct your own interviews and check references, regardless of where you receive names or who makes recommendations.

Locating an in-house caregiver is frequently time consuming,
emotionally wrenching, and physically difficult. If you exhaust all
possibilities, you might want to consider other options. For example, some parents use two part-time placements each week. Or
you might need to offer extra services, like transportation.

You might also need to be more flexible than you originally
intended. For example, moms who participated in a national sur-
vey reported that these elements were critical in finding a caregiver: safety, communication with parents, cleanliness, warmth
toward children, attention given to children, style of discipline,
and experience. Compare this list with the qualities you are seeking in a caregiver. You might find it's not essential to have someone
come to your home. It may be possible to have your baby in a
safe, loving, caring environment away from your home.

❧ ❧ ❧ ❧ ❧ ❧ ❧

Q What kind of baby shower gift could I buy for someone who already has a three year old and a one year old?

A Instead of buying something for the new baby, plan something to help the family. Here are a few options:

• Try food. Prepare a meal, complete with muffins or sweet breads even the one year old could eat. Schedule the meal for the third day home from the hospital or later. There's lots of help (sometimes too much) the first day home.

Or, buy a supermarket gift certificate or fast-food restaurant coupon book. Or, make up a fresh fruit basket, including bananas or other fruits the one year old can eat. Add a bow to a stack of small fruit juice cans. Those little cans are handy to grab when a child needs something quick while Mom is preoccupied with the new baby, and they're great for the new mother, too.

• Offer time. Plan together when you can care for the two older children one morning. Or, offer a stroller ride for one or two children around the block, once each day for a week, perhaps from 4:30-5:00 P.M. (This is often the toughest time of day.)

• Give reading material. Order a subscription to a children's or parent's magazine.

• Give yourself. Perhaps you can watch the older kids and do some cleanup or laundry while the mother and baby take a nap. But if there isn't a real need for your help right now, the biggest and best gift would be not staying too long to visit after the birth. I usually arrive at newborn visits with a basket of nutritious snacks, a few toys for the older children, and a timer for me. That helps me respect the needs of the new baby's family.

❧ ❧ ❧ ❧ ❧ ❧ ❧

Q *I love my new baby very much, but so far being a mom hasn't been what I wanted. I don't know what's wrong with me, but it's just so different from what I thought it would be.*

A Please don't be too hard on yourself. It can be shocking to compare real life "after baby" with the magazine covers showing well-rested moms with pre-baby figures holding baby powder-fresh, perfectly dressed cherubs.

Since giving birth, you've already done a lot of things and learned a lot, too. Remember that you are growing up with your baby. Don't expect to know everything right away; do expect to keep learning. That pattern will continue for many, many years, so give yourself some time.

Each stage of parenting has special joys and challenges. Focus on the moment: when you hold your baby as she falls asleep, when she gurgles at you, when she stares intently at the world around her.

Identify things about mothering now that make you smile or give you a sense of peace. Then celebrate! You might even want to jot down your feelings and experiences in a little journal. Date every entry.

Media images and expectations of perfection can wear you down, but it doesn't need to be that way. There will be new experiences to enjoy in the future, but take this first season of parenting, and each one that follows, a single day at a time.

❦ ❦ ❦ ❦ ❦ ❦ ❦

Q Will my baby be smarter if I read to him?

A Not necessarily. I cannot guarantee that if you read to your baby now he will be able to read earlier or score higher on an achievement test than your neighbor's child.

However, reading offers quality bonding time in an environment rich with language. A baby also learns the pre-reading concepts that books are fun, that you turn pages to see different pictures, that books are held right-side up, and that you read from front to back. Because reading books with you is associated with a pleasant time of cuddles, attention, interesting sounds, and colorful pictures, you are helping him take the first step to becoming a lifetime reader. Literacy is associated with many characteristics of "successful" people.

Reading to your child can begin very naturally when your baby is about six months old, because by that time he can hold up his head without it wobbling too much. Look for books made from heavy cardboard ("board books"). Cloth and plastic books will hold up even if your teething baby develops a "taste" for literature.

❦ ❦ ❦ ❦ ❦ ❦ ❦

Q How many covers should I use on my baby?

A Newborns are the only ones who generally need to be kept warmer than normal. Otherwise, dress your baby as you dress yourself. Avoid overdressing. When the weather is cool, make sure to cover your baby's head.

❦ ❦ ❦ ❦ ❦ ❦ ❦

How do I know if the baby-sitter is changing my baby's diaper often enough?

Before the sitter comes again, note how many diapers you use in a morning, afternoon, and evening. That will give you a basis to compare your habits with the sitter's. If the sitter watches your baby in your own home, empty the diaper pail before you leave. Note the number and heaviness of used diapers when you return. If you bring the baby to the sitter, track how often the sitter requests that you bring more diapers.

You might decide the baby-sitter should change the baby more often; ask the sitter to do so. Usually a diaper is changed at feeding time or other times when fussing indicates a new diaper is needed. Cloth diapers need more frequent changing because wetness stays next to your baby's skin. If your baby develops a rash, the diaper should be changed more often.

❦ ❦ ❦ ❦ ❦ ❦ ❦

I had my baby three months ago but can't seem to get my energy back. Do you have any suggestions?

First check with your obstetrician. After an exam to be sure your body is all right, your doctor will probably remind you that it might take a long time to regain your energy. I breathed a sigh of relief when my obstetrician said, "Add up the months you've breast-fed and the nine months of pregnancy. That's how long it will take until your body is back to being itself." Of course, some of us need more time than that!

Here are some other suggestions:

• Don't expect to be a supermom. I have spoken to thousands of parents. Although I've never met a superparent, I've met lots of people who almost kill themselves trying to fit that image. Don't put yourself into that category.

• Sleep or nap frequently. Lie down when your baby lies down.

• Say "no" to all commitments; say "yes" to all offers of help (and don't waste valuable energy on feeling guilty).

• Conserve your strength. Use convenience foods. Prioritize household jobs. Do only what's absolutely necessary.

• Build a support group. Phone your hospital roommate, ask your Lamaze teacher to set up a reunion for your class, or attend a meeting of the LaLeche League, MOPS (Mothers of Preschoolers), or another group that includes new moms. Find out what they're doing and how they're doing.

• Focus on your job: caring for a newborn. You are learning how to be a mother and bonding with your baby. That's a full-time job.

🐛 🐛 🐛 🐛 🐛 🐛 🐛

Q *What can I do when people say, "Oh, what a darling baby" and totally ignore my three year old?*

A Draw attention to your older child and also give her positive verbal feedback. You might use one of these lines:

• "Thank you. Now that I'm so busy I especially appreciate Brooke being my special helper. She's so good at . . ."

• "I remember when Brooke was this little and she liked . . ."

• "Thanks, and you should see how Brooke can get him to smile. Brooke has a special way of making me smile, too."

❦ ❦ ❦ ❦ ❦ ❦ ❦

Q I'm a new mother, and I don't want to do anything wrong. I worry a lot. If I'm this worried now, I'll be a nervous wreck when my child's older!

A Relax. When you don't know what to do, consult a book like this one or talk with a friend. But most of all, trust your own instincts.

Even if your baby was born just last week, you are the expert on her. You've already learned what comforts her and what bothers her. You've learned in what position she prefers to sleep. You know more about your baby than anyone else. You also know yourself. Have confidence in your ability to parent.

I'm not saying that parenting can't be scary. It is, regardless of how old your child is.

I'm also not implying that you shouldn't think about what you do as a parent. People who think about their parenting will be more effective parents. Wise parents know that experience isn't the best teacher—learning from experience is the best teacher.

Of course, your daughter needs your smiles, songs, and caresses. She needs to be fed and changed and dressed properly. She craves a safe, warm, comfortable environment. If you're giving her these things, you're doing a good job as a mom.

I can tell you from experience that it doesn't help to worry about the future. Remember that your baby isn't going to be the only one growing up. You'll be growing up with her. When she is a five year old, you'll not only be five years older, but you'll have the potential to be five years wiser.

Q *I know the answer to this question is "yes," but will I ever again sleep through the night? Our son is nine months old.*

A The good news is: Yes, some night you will sleep the whole night. The bad news is that sleep deprivation is part of every stage of parenting. The parent of a four year old might sleep fitfully, listening to a croupy child; the parent of a teen doesn't sleep until the front door clicks open at midnight. At every stage, take one day at a time and grab every bit of rest that's possible.

If you need help now, here are some ideas:

• Call a friend. Take turns caring for each other's children sometime during the day so you'll get a free hour.

• Lie down when your son naps (if he ever does).

• Hire an older student to care for your baby for an hour or two every day after school. Even if you don't sleep, the rest will be helpful.

• Prioritize what you must do; forget everything else.

❧ ❧ ❧ ❧ ❧ ❧ ❧

Q *My daughter is sixteen months old. How do I teach her to pray?*

A Every day your daughter is probably trying out a new word or sound, so this is a good age to start talking to God. Build prayer into daily routines. Begin be praying before meals, at naptime, and at bedtime. Prayers will be simple and probably very short. You might say at mealtime, "Thank you, Jesus," and soon your daughter can add, "Amen." This is typically a favorite word for toddlers. A month from now, you might add the words, "Thank you, Jesus, for food." Soon your daughter might echo the words or say them with you. Look for prayer opportunities that might not happen daily: you might pray before driving to

Grandma's or while bundling up your daughter for a stroller ride.

Through thank-you prayers and "gimme" prayers, your daughter will learn two important concepts: God will listen to prayer anytime, and she can talk to God. And because many lullabies are really prayers in the form of cradle songs, she will also learn that prayer takes several forms.

Toddlers love to copy actions, so this is a good time to show your daughter how to fold or lift her hands to the Lord.

And most of all, remember her daily in your own prayers.

🍎 🍎 🍎 🍎 🍎 🍎 🍎

Q *Will my toddler learn faster if I use baby talk like "bobby" for bottle, "nappie" for nap, and "blankie" for blanket?*

A Clear communication is the goal of our talking. By using context clues and visual clues, a toddler comprehends at least some of what we are saying.

Use correct vocabulary and grammar right from the beginning. Then your child won't need to relearn basic language when he's older.

🍎 🍎 🍎 🍎 🍎 🍎 🍎

Q *My daughter just started walking, and I'm finally enjoying being a mother. Why did it take me so long to like being a parent?*

A You've discovered something parents seldom admit: Different people are more effective or happier parents at different stages of their child's development. For example, I loved nursing my cuddly little babies and enjoyed watching my teenagers become adults; I struggled through the junior-high years. You and I don't parent evenly through the seasons of a child's life, so your experience is very normal.

Look for the positives as you go through your daughter's childhood years. Each stage of parenting will have special joys and challenges.

Q My daughter is only seventeen months old, but she's acting like a "terrible two." I know she's smart, but is she that far ahead?

A Although some people talk about the "terrible twos," child development experts indicate the time just before and after age two (eighteen months and then two and a half years) is the really rough period. Textbook writers call this a time of "natural disequilibrium."

See if this sounds familiar: Your daughter wants to be independent but doesn't want to be independent. She wants to stay at Mother's Day Out but doesn't want to leave you. She wants to cuddle her blue lamb; then no, she wants to play with her stacking toy. At this time, your daughter is moving backward and forward, often simultaneously. These are typical situations.

Because she will frequently test boundaries and her behavior will be full of contradictions, be especially clear and consistent when you set limits.

Q My daughter is two and a half, but she is still in the "terrible twos." Could I have done something to prevent this stage? We'd like another child, and I don't want to go through this again.

A Some tough times are preventable; others, like this stage, are part of normal development. Some children seem to fight their way through each level; other children have relatively calm behavior throughout the early years.

During times of potential stress, pay special attention to your own physical needs and state of mind. You'll cope more effectively with your child when you eat properly and are well rested.

Q Is it bad to let my eighteen-month-old son watch television in the morning while I get dressed for work?

A No, not as long as you are aware of two things: that the television is serving as a baby-sitter, and that programming and commercials can both influence your son.

I assume you have selected appropriate programs. You have limited the use of television to a certain time each day. You're using TV as a tool to meet your needs as a parent and to provide positive stimulation for your son. These elements all combine to offer an excellent example of how to use television in a positive way.

Also consider other at-home baby-sitting aids: cassette/book sets, books, puppets, puzzles, activity kits, and tapes. All of these items will involve your child physically and mentally. When you use television in addition to these other activities, you are putting TV in its proper place: one of many leisure-time options for your son.

Q An older man frowned at me in church when I pulled out dry cereal for my one and a half year old yesterday. Isn't it all right to take snacks and toys?

A Yes. A survival kit is helpful for parents of young children. Small toys, coloring books and crayons, quiet books, and a bag of dry cereal are good to carry to church, the doctor's office, or any place where children can't be as active as they might be. You might pack a church bag with Bible story books and Bible action figures, or play items purchased from the local Christian bookstore.

A survival kit says you are planning ahead to meet your child's needs and to prevent problems. That's good for everyone. Even older children tend to have more positive experiences when they take books or hand-held games to places that require waiting or extended quiet behavior. The only thing that changes through the years is that children gradually move into packing their own bags and selecting their own items, until they developmentally adopt adult-type behaviors in confined settings.

❦ ❦ ❦ ❦ ❦ ❦ ❦

Q How can I get my two year old to put toys into the toy box and not just take things out?

A I suggest you get rid of the toy box. It not only has the potential of becoming a safety hazard, but it usually becomes a junk box. A two year old can learn that everything has a place. Unfortunately, even the neatest toy box doesn't communicate that.

Instead, buy or build a simple shelf unit. Sort your child's toys into clear plastic storage bins or empty shoe boxes, if you prefer. Have a separate box for each type of toy: blocks, stacking toys, small cars, and so on.

Involve your child in sorting and organizing the items. Get rid of anything that is broken or "almost" works. Then, label each bin with a word and/or a picture and line up the bins on the shelf. Set two basic rules with your child: 1. Use one box at a time. 2. Put the box away before taking out another.

As your child grows up, change the rule to fit his new abilities and interests. For example, next year your two year old might want to make a road for trucks, so he'll need two bins. A couple months later, he might want to add people.

Once the system is set up, invest some time in playing with your child over the next several days, so you can model and positively reinforce these guidelines.

Q *Does my baby need a bath every day?*

A Probably not, as long as the diaper area is kept clean. However, you can consider scheduling a daily bath time even though it might not be essential from a medical standpoint.

Tub time each day can be an excellent family building block. Families need the consistency of an activity that happens regularly. You might pray aloud in the car when you drop your baby off at the baby-sitter each day before work; six months from now, you might read your child a board book after supper every night. These are examples of family building blocks. You've probably already learned that routines are important, even to an infant. A daily bath, and the associated play and cuddling time, might be one building block for your family during these early years.

Q *How can I encourage, but not force, my two and a half year old to learn?*

A First, because of individual differences between parents and children, what is stressful to one child might be perceived as just the right level of support for another child. Also, you will face this issue many times during the next few years. Although you may answer this judgment call in different ways at various times, here are some general guidelines:

• Combine planned and spontaneous experiences. Schedule a picnic in the park, but also stop to talk about a dead bird on the sidewalk.

• Offer lots of real-life learning experiences. Be wary of pencil-and-paper tasks or workbooks; a two year old needs to pet a goat, not just "put an X on each goat in the picture." In later years you can balance formal programs and real experiences.

• Be especially cautious of programs that promise to accelerate normal growth and development, for example, "Teach your toddler to read in ten days." I support surrounding your child with books, but preschoolers need to discover the joy of reading, not a system of decoding.

• Observe your child. Watch how she responds to various situations. Young learners are relaxed, excited, and sometimes intense and focused, but they shouldn't show signs of anxiety, which might include nail-biting or sleep problems.

• Share with your child. If you go to the zoo together or attend your child's play group, you will see firsthand how she learns most effectively.

• Follow your instincts. Ask yourself, "What feels right?" Often, if you pay attention to your own parent-sense, you'll make the best decision.

🐌 🐌 🐌 🐌 🐌 🐌 🐌

Q *Is there a difference between a child-care center, an enrichment center, and a child-development center?*

A Yes, according to textbook definitions. However, in practice, these and other terms are used interchangeably.

More important than a name is what happens at the site, who the providers are, and whether or not the program meets the needs of your child.

One thing that's worth looking for in a name are the words *NAEYC Accredited.* The National Association for the Education for Young Children (NAEYC) has an excellent system of accreditation. Centers that hold this ranking have completed a major self-study and meet minimum requirements in a wide variety of areas of importance. Contact NAEYC (800-424-2460) if you would like the names of accredited sites in your region.

But remember, regardless of a name or title, the single most important thing when seeking child care is if the site and personnel will be good for your child. And you—not a neighbor or a national organization—are the best judge of that.

Chapter Two

Early Childhood
THREE TO FOUR YEARS OLD

* Back to diapers
* Sad paintings
* Ugly art
* Encouraging quiet child
* "Why?"
* Questions about death
* Attending a funeral
* Day care challenging?
* Three year old "reads"
* Why so afraid?
* No more blankies
* Day care rut?
* Sharing
* Hates lessons
* No time to answer
* Resists spiritual leading
* Block building

* Cutting with scissors
* Sex questions
* Fishing
* Hates own bed
* "No"
* Who needs preschool?
* "Just" play
* Pre-K good preparation?
* Frequent moves
* Fat pencil
* Reading before kindergarten
* Teaching to read
* Preparing for kindergarten
* Prayer

Q My three year old, who was out of diapers very successfully months ago, has been having at least one accident a day. I think he's just lazy. How can I motivate him to stay dry?

A This is a fairly common situation for parents of three or four year olds, although that doesn't reduce your frustration level. Sometimes, preschoolers have wet bottoms simply because they don't want to interrupt play.

First, phone your physician to see if your son should be checked for an infection.

If your son is physically all right, a simple sticker chart is often an effective motivator. ("You get a sticker each time you go to the bathroom. When the chart is filled, you can invite a friend to lunch at McDonald's.")

Continue to emphasize the positive. Don't give a lot of attention to the accidents. Soon, peers will probably apply enough indirect pressure that your son will want to stay dry all the time.

🐛 🐛 🐛 🐛 🐛 🐛 🐛

Q My three year old paints at day care, but his paintings are all very dark. Could he be depressed or unhappy?

A Talk with your child-care provider if you're concerned, but dark paintings alone don't necessarily indicate depression. Dark paint might be all that's available when he gets to the easel. Or, your son might only like the kind of brushes that are in the dark paint. Or, your son simply might like dark colors for the next few weeks.

Preschoolers go through many phases: a child might play with blocks every day for a month, or spend a lot of time doing puzzles for a few weeks. Your son is probably just at the stage of dark paint.

❧ ❧ ❧ ❧ ❧ ❧ ❧

Q How can I be kind to my three-year-old son when he brings home artwork that is ugly?

A Respond honestly. Give specific comments. Say something positive. Here are examples:

• Look for something good. For example, "I like the way you used orange. You know that's one of my favorite colors."

• Don't assume you know what he painted or drew unless it's clear. If you aren't certain, say, "Tell me about this."

• Emphasize what's important: the process is often more important than the product during the early-childhood years. If he enjoyed being an artist, that might be all that matters. You might ask, "What was the best part of painting today?" or "Should we mail this to Grandma? She might want to see how much you liked to paint today."

❧ ❧ ❧ ❧ ❧ ❧ ❧

Q How can I get my three-year-old daughter to talk more?

A I'll answer by asking you questions. Does your daughter need to talk? Is an older sibling answering for her? Do you anticipate her every need? Some children don't talk because they don't need to talk. It's tempting to jump in during a lull in the conversation, but hold yourself back and tune into your daughter's speech pace. Wait for her to ask for a second cookie or a glass of water.

Some children are naturally quiet, and that's fine. But if you'd like to increase vocabulary development and frequency of speech, enrich the language environment by taking these steps:

1. Use the word version of "surround sound." Simply talk about everyday experiences as they happen. For example, when you walk through the produce department at the grocery store, you might say, "Let's look for the head of lettuce that feels heaviest. You find one and I'll find one and we'll see which weighs the most." Look for opportunities like this to weave conversation naturally into everything you do. "Small talk" like this will happen most easily if the television is turned off.

2. Designate talking time. Set aside one or two specific times each day when you will talk. Often this works well at bedtime, before naps, or after supper. This is also an ideal time to read books, listen together to stories on tape, or sing songs. You can incorporate many forms of language into a loosely labeled "talking time." If you set aside these regular times when your child is three years old, you'll have an excellent pattern to continue throughout her growing-up years.

If you don't notice significant speech and language growth, sit near the sandbox when your daughter is playing with friends. If she uses significantly less language than her peers, talk with your pediatrician, who might suggest seeing an audiologist for a hearing evaluation. Also, consult your medical practitioner if your daughter has had frequent ear infections, as this can sometimes delay language.

Q Why does a three year old ask so many "why" questions?

A Preschoolers ask a lot of "why" and "how come" questions because that's their natural way to learn about the world around them.

Your answers give a lot of important information. Encourage creative thinking by answering "why" questions with your own question, "Why do you think?"

You will face "why" questions through many seasons of parenting. Whenever possible, view these questions as an opportunity to teach.

❧ ❧ ❧ ❧ ❧ ❧ ❧

Q *My inquisitive three and a half year old has been asking questions like, "Where is heaven?", "What do people do in heaven?", "What does it mean to be dead?" How do I honestly explain the finality of death without frightening her?*

A A preschooler can't really understand the final nature of death. But your truthful and direct approach says, "Come to me with your questions. I will tell you what I know and believe."

Her questions offer an excellent opportunity to share your religious convictions. Ask your daughter's Sunday-school teacher or Christian-education director for some guidance. Also, check your church or public library for books on death and dying issues that are written for very young children. As you talk, you are not only answering her questions, but reinforcing that she is safe talking with you about important issues. You are also communicating that you will help her learn about concepts that are hard to understand. Questions about death will reappear at various points during your daughter's childhood.

❧ ❧ ❧ ❧ ❧ ❧ ❧

Q *Was I right to leave my three year old at home with a sitter when I went to a funeral? I thought he was too young to understand what was happening.*

A I probably would have done the same thing. A three year old cannot understand that death is forever. In addition, your son might have become restless after sitting very quietly for a long period of time in a solemn atmosphere. Although that's normal for a young child, his behavior could have been distracting to others in this situation.

🐛 🐛 🐛 🐛 🐛 🐛 🐛

Q *My son is so much smarter than the other kids at his day care that I wonder if he's learning anything.*

A It's good you're looking at what your son can get from the experience. Reexamine the goals you set for your son's daycare experience. Are those goals being met? Is your son happy? Is he having positive experiences?

If you answered "yes" to all those questions, then it appears the center is a good match for your son at this time. If your son is continuing to grow, he has already learned a valuable lesson: a good teacher doesn't necessarily need to be older or smarter than a student, but a student should be open to learning from many sources. A child can learn many important skills and shape lifelong attitudes when surrounded by peers. While your son teaches another child how to use a measuring cup (cognitive learning), that child might show your son how to wait patiently during a game (social-emotional learning.)

🐛 🐛 🐛 🐛 🐛 🐛 🐛

Q *My three year old "reads" because she has memorized the story. She doesn't turn the pages at the right time and doesn't want my help to match the right words to the right page. Is it okay to just let her "read"?*

A Yes. Your daughter is doing a great job in a number of pre-reading areas.

She's holding the book right-side up, she's turning the pages from front to back, and she's probably even moving her eyes along the page from left to right. These are all important aspects of the early reading process that we often don't even notice.

And it's fine that she moves through books at her own pace. As she begins to identify letters, or even familiar words, she'll gradually match her "reading" to the correct pages.

What's most important, though, is that she likes books and enjoys her own kind of reading.

$$\text{\it s \hspace{0.2em} s \hspace{0.2em} s \hspace{0.2em} s \hspace{0.2em} s \hspace{0.2em} s \hspace{0.2em} s}$$

Q *Why would my three year old be afraid of a new baby elephant when he saw one at the zoo?*

A Perhaps for the same reason one of my children was afraid of balloons or another preschooler is afraid of gerbils.

Sometimes young children have fears that appear totally out-of-nowhere and seem irrational to us. However, we need to respect the fears of a young child because they are very real. Reassure your child that you will protect him and that he is safe.

Sometime in the future, if you're reading an animal book that includes some pictures or a story about elephants, you might casually ask if he'd like to see an elephant sometime; however, this is not something to push. Fears like these generally decrease over a period of months or years as children grow older.

Q After the Christmas break, my daughter's teacher won't let students bring toys or blankies or anything like that to preschool. My daughter carries a stuffed animal every day. Now, my daughter doesn't want to go back to preschool, and I'm stuck.

A I haven't seen specific research to document this, but my observation shows that separation from a security object usually follows a pattern: the child needs it everywhere, the child needs it at specific times or places, the child starts to "forget" he needs it, and the child doesn't miss it or realizes he doesn't need it. Peer pressure ("You're still carrying that old elephant?") dramatically stops dependency situations.

Your daughter's teacher should take cues from the students on moments of "readiness" for the next stage of emotional growth. This is important because individual timetables vary.

Ask the teacher for suggestions. After all, you both want your daughter to feel good about herself, school, and the world around her. The most natural way to do that is to respect her needs and encourage developmentally appropriate growth. For example, the preschool teacher might allow your daughter to bring the animal out only for storytime. Or, the teacher might have observed that the animal stays in the cubbie all day, and bringing the toy appears to have outlived its usefulness. Dialog with the teacher so you work through this dilemma as partners who care about your child.

❧ ❧ ❧ ❧ ❧ ❧ ❧

Q Is it bad to keep a child in the same day-care center for three years?

A No. Having the same environment can provide a tremendous sense of security for a young child. If your son enters a center and indicates it "feels like home," that's one sign of a good fit for him. Part of that feeling might come with the familiarity of the setting and primary caregivers.

But it's good you're alert to the potential problems with the same year-round child-care setting. Children can become bored in a stagnant environment.

Talk with your son's teacher about the plans for his continued learning. Good care includes a caregiver who is responsive to your son's continued growth and development.

Q *How do I encourage, but not force, my child to share?*

A We plant the seeds of sharing during the preschool years. It takes two to make a seesaw work. Children can string beads together from opposite ends. Two young children can take a walk together, both pushing their own lawn mower or doll carriage.

Setting up possibilities for sharing—without pushing it to happen—can be low-key ways for helping our children grow as sharing people. Words and positive body language can draw attention to times when your child shares.

Q *My three year old hates swimming lessons so much that every class is a struggle. Should I stop taking him?*

A Think back to the reasons you signed him up for the class. Are those goals being met? Are those goals realistic for your child? If you work out this situation on paper, you will probably see that there are many ways to meet those original goals. For example:

Goal: Teach basic water safety.

Ways to meet the goal:

1. Sign him up for swimming class.

2. Teach him swimming safety rules yourself: Walk on deck— no running. Wear a bubble. Stay out of the water until a parent is with you.

Goal: Meet other children.

Ways to meet the goal:

1. Sign him up for swimming lessons or kids gym.

2. Take him to Sunday school or Teddy Bear Time at the library.

3. Set up a play group.

If your first attempt at meeting a goal doesn't seem to work, return to your worksheet for another alternative. This one might be a winner!

❧ ❧ ❧ ❧ ❧ ❧ ❧

Q What book should I use to teach my three year old to read?

A You can use every children's book in the library. That's because we help our children most by reading to them, letting them page through books, encouraging them to dictate stories to us, and exposing them to all kinds of reading material and experiences.

There isn't a single book I'd recommend for teaching children to read. I'm not against young children reading, but I have two concerns.

Some young children are pushed (parents tend to use the word "encouraged") to sit down and work on reading-related skills long before they are ready. Regardless of how bright a child is, it's not developmentally right for a preschooler to use flash cards.

Another too-common sight is a young child who can read (understand that symbols represent words and decode these symbols) but who doesn't know how to share, handle a paint brush, or develop a true friendship. The tragedy is not children who learn to read early, but those who learn only to read.

It's great you are eager to help your child. Take your child to story hours at the library. Check out a lot of books. Page through children's magazines together, talking about the pictures, ideas, and concepts. Identify all the signs you see on a walk around the neighborhood. In a year or two, your child might want to find familiar letters and words on the cereal box at breakfast. Let your child tell favorite stories into a tape recorder.

If you do all that, you will truly help your child learn to read.

🐦 🐦 🐦 🐦 🐦 🐦 🐦

Q *Whenever we get ready to go somewhere or when I'm trying to work, my three and a half year old asks me questions that I don't have time to answer. Is she doing this for attention, because she always pulls this trick when I'm busy?*

A Possibly. Children are often well-behaved until we become unavailable in situations like the ones you've described.

The next time this happens, jot down the question on a piece of paper, and tell your daughter what you're doing. Say, "I can't answer your question right now. I'm going to write it down. Then, when we get in the car, I will answer it."

Be certain to follow through with the answer. This will show that your daughter's question is important but that the timing isn't right.

❧ ❧ ❧ ❧ ❧ ❧ ❧

Q *What do we do with a three and a half year old who seems resistant to our spiritual leading?*

A As a preschooler, your son is expressing a very young faith in his own way. Even the most compliant young child will not do everything perfectly all of the time. Many children, at one time or another, complain about boring devotions, cause a disruption in church, or mutter prayers.

Give your son some space and time to grow as a child of God. As you do that, though, continue your efforts in spiritual nurture. Let your child see the bookmark move in your Bible. Include your child in mealtime prayers. Relate faith to the daily Christian walk. And don't underestimate the power of God in your son's life or the witness you are giving.

The whole burden of spiritual nurture isn't on your shoulders: God is with you now. God will continue to work through you and others to bring your son closer to Him. God will be faithful to you in your calling as a Christian parent.

❧ ❧ ❧ ❧ ❧ ❧ ❧

Q *What's wrong with my son? Other kids at day care build big buildings with blocks, but my boy just piles blocks on top of each other.*

A If your son interacts well with other children and is involved in play throughout the day, it's quite possible there's nothing wrong.

It sounds like your son is enjoying what he's doing; that's fine. That's what play is all about. Children who haven't had a lot of experience with blocks build simpler structures. There are stages of block building, and your son might stay for quite a while at this level of block building.

If you'd like to give him more block building experience, find pieces of scrap wood at the local lumber yard. You and your son could spend some time sanding the wood to make your own blocks. Then keep the blocks handy for your son to use. He might want to add some little cars and small people from a play set. But please don't push your son to "Build me a house." He will do that when he's ready.

Q *How can I teach my four year old to cut?*

A Children gradually learn how to cut, usually after several years of experience. Some first graders have trouble cutting properly, so please don't expect too much from your four year old.

You might encourage some informal pre-scissors games:

Fill the sink with a bubble bath or with plain water. Your child might like to play in the water with a clean turkey baster. This is excellent practice in opening and closing his hands.

Ask your child to serve the tossed salad. Using salad tongs will give him practice opening and closing a tool, similar to the movement needed for scissors. Plan to ask your child to do this before people sit down to eat, so he can try it privately. When people are seated, it's easy to accent the positive: "Jeremy served the salad for us already. He used the big salad tongs."

Next, let your child use a paper punch. This adds one more task: now your child will not only open and close the tool, but also hold the paper. He could pretend to be a train conductor, punching tickets for all his stuffed-animal passengers.

Once your child is really interested in using the scissors, he'll enjoy clipping coupons from the newspaper. Or, he might want to fringe the edges of a piece of construction paper for a placemat.

Cutting straight lines comes before cutting curved lines. But remember, using scissors isn't easy. Assist informally. Give a lot of encouragement, and avoid pushing him to cut before he's truly ready for this task.

Q *My four year old is starting to ask questions about sex. Where do I start?*

A Begin where your child left off: with his questions. For example, a usual first question is, "Where did I come from?" You can approach the answer to this or other basic questions about sex in two different ways:

1. Use a question: "Where do you think you came from?"

Your child's response will tell you what your child already knows. This is important, because when it comes to sex, children generally have some information and some misinformation.

2. Begin with the simplest response: "You were born at Memorial Hospital. Is that what you wanted to know?"

The first statement gives your child basic information. Adding that extra question is an easy way to find out if you've answered your child's question.

Q *My father wants to take my four year old fishing, but isn't she too young?*

A There's no need to rush a child into an activity when safety concerns, because of her age, might overshadow enjoyment.

However, if Grandpa can view this strictly as a teaching opportunity for his granddaughter instead of as a fishing trip for him, they can probably have a happy time.

Your daughter will need to understand the importance of following rules and obeying directions. Begin by role-playing every aspect of the trip. Make a "pretend" boat in the living room or backyard. Simply lay out a piece of string for the outline of the boat. Or ask your child to outline a boat with blocks.

Help her put on the life preserver she will wear. Find a secure-fitting hat that won't blow off but will protect her eyes from glare off the water.

State basic safety rules before getting in the "boat." She must clearly understand the meaning of "Don't stand up" and "Don't swing your hook around." Get a bright colored cushion or towel for your daughter to sit on in the boat—when she sees that, she will know exactly where she should be. Help her practice getting into the "boat."

Then she can practice lowering a hookless line. Some experts recommend getting a child's starter set or using a bamboo pole with a bobber. Throughout this rehearsal, Grandpa will need to consistently stress safety, just as he will do during the big fishing trip.

If your daughter will fish off a bank, give your dad a piece of red yarn to lay on the shore. This will show your daughter how close to the water she can stand. Your father might need to put the line into the water, simply because of your daughter's limited ability to control all her directional muscle activity.

Before the trip, ask Grandpa to show pictures of his "big catches." Some young children are crushed to learn that "those cute little fish" (minnows) get eaten up or that squiggly worms become food for fish. This is a natural way to learn about the food chain, but not all four year olds enjoy this aspect, so share this information in advance.

During this practice session, if there is any indication that your daughter (or her grandfather) is not ready for fishing, postpone the trip until your child is older.

$ $ $ $ $ $ $

Q How do I handle my four-year-old son at night when he wants to sleep in my bed?

A A common solution is to offer a cuddle, a night light, and an extra prayer. Or, you might want to develop another way to assure your child he's safe and secure. For example, you might sit on the floor by the bed and sing songs until he dozes off. Or, turn on a sleepytime tape. Because there are many "right" solutions, use your best judgment. Just be loving and consistent with whatever you choose to do.

Gradually, the "I want to sleep in your bed" concern will fade away. However, months from now, your son might repeat his request. This bedtime issue typically emerges at various times throughout childhood.

$ $ $ $ $ $ $

Q My four and a half year old breaks into a crying fit whenever I say "no." It can be "no" to a snack five minutes before supper or "no" to going to play at a friend's house or anything else she doesn't like.

A For several days, keep track of when the tantrums happen. Then add this new information to what you already know about your child. Tantrums often occur when a child has not received adequate warning of a change about to happen, she's hungry, she's tired, or she hasn't had a hug or attention from you for a while.

For example, perhaps she is especially cranky right after she gets up in the morning. Because you are the expert on your child, you know the morning routines will go more smoothly if she eats first. Or, if she gets cranky about midmorning, you know she might need a snack.

One of the most common mistakes we make as parents is forgetting our children need time for transitions. For example, any child might throw a fit if the castle she's been building all morning is almost done and she needs to stop because "Lunch is ready." Instead, it would be better to alert the child that, "Lunch will be ready in ten minutes. Finish what you're doing."

As you seek to eliminate opportunities for the tantrums, also be consistent in your response. When your daughter throws a tantrum, simply walk away. Do this every single time, as long as she can't hurt herself or someone else. Some children act up simply to get attention, even if the attention is negative.

Q *Should all kids go to preschool? I'm not sure if I should send my daughter.*

A No, not all children need preschool, and your daughter might be one of them. The needs of young children can be met efficiently at home. Here's what a preschool-aged child needs:

• Socially: opportunities to play with children her own age, practice sharing, and act out roles in dramatic play. She should experience winning and losing, and learn to get along with others.

• Emotionally: a chance to talk about her feelings, identify how she feels at different times, and grow in a warm, positive environment. Feedback and experiences should produce many opportunities for her to feel good about who she is, how she is growing, and what she is learning.

• Mentally: exposure to many books, places, people, and things. She should be surrounded by spoken and printed language and encouraged to learn through active participation. She should count, classify, and be urged to talk about everything.

• Physically: the opportunity to use small and large muscles. That means she should draw with chalk on the sidewalk, use her finger to write her name in the sandbox, work puzzles, put together blocks, swing, play catch, and walk around the block.

• Spiritually: the opportunity to learn Bible stories, pray, regularly participate in worship and church activities, and watch you practice forgiveness.

❧ ❧ ❧ ❧ ❧ ❧ ❧

Q I peeked into my son's preschool the other day, and all they were doing was playing. He loves the preschool, and I really like the teacher. But I'm paying for more than play, aren't I? Should I find a new preschool?

A First, I don't believe it's good for young children to sit with a pencil, paper, and workbook pages. If you're "paying for play" that is rich in language and experiences, then your money is well-invested. If your child has a chance to build a tall tower with another child, spend ten minutes at the easel, look through a magnifying glass, watch fish swim, pour water through a funnel, type on a keyboard, listen to a story, or ride a truck, you have found a wonderful place.

Before you change preschools, ask the teacher when you can visit for part of a day. Look carefully at what's happening. Ask yourself, "Does my child seem happy? Is he relaxed and comfortable? How is he benefiting from his time here?"

After your observation ask the teacher about developmentally appropriate activities for young children. Find out why play is a priority. Ask how your son benefits from measuring beans, building a card tower, or playing restaurant.

It's not always easy to measure how much a child learns through doing, but we do know that young children learn the most in a home or classroom that respects play as a driving force.

🍎 🍎 🍎 🍎 🍎 🍎 🍎

Q *I know pre-kindergarten is a time to play with other children, but will my son be prepared for real school next year?*

A Your son has not only been learning how to share, cooperate, and solve problems, but in pre-kindergarten he also has been learning many things related to school readiness:

• He has practiced visual tracking, or following a moving object with his eyes while controlling it with his hands. That has happened when he's driven a play tractor over a farm road he's built with blocks.

• He's laying the groundwork for understanding the set theory in mathematics. This has happened when he has put plastic vegetables in the refrigerator, fruits in the fruit bowl, and empty dry-cereal boxes in the cupboard.

• He has learned many important reading concepts. When he asked the teacher to "Make a sign that says *garage*," he watched how the teacher formed the letters going from left to right, and he realized that letters stand for something.

Perhaps your son will be printing his name next fall—many kindergarteners do. Maybe he will be able to count out twenty napkins for the snack. If so, that's great. But you can't rush the readiness process. Young children need caring adults to help them interpret their early experiences. Preschoolers need to pump on a swing and learn to tell someone how they feel. That's what your son should be doing right now.

If your son enters kindergarten being able to tell another child, "I'm mad at you for stepping on my toe," instead of hitting the child; if he shows sensitivity to a child who bumped his head; if he approaches story time with eagerness and curiosity, any kindergarten teacher will welcome your son and will be grateful to have a student who truly is ready to continue learning in developmentally appropriate ways.

❧ ❧ ❧ ❧ ❧ ❧ ❧

Q *We are in the military. How will frequent moves affect our children?*

A After the very early years of life, any move has the potential to cause major disruption to a child's normal life patterns.

This shouldn't come as any surprise: we all feel most comfortable with what we know. But children, simply because of their level of development, don't have the intellectual ability to project to the future or understand the meaning of a long-term adjustment. Children live in the here and now; when that changes, their world is turned upside down.

There can be significant benefits to relocation: a child has a chance to start over, make new friends, be exposed to new cultures and learning situations. At one time or another, many of us would probably welcome the chance to start with a fresh slate.

However, because of the many upheavals that occur simultaneously with a move, even small episodes can appear overwhelming to a child.

Q *Must my son use a fat pencil to learn how to print correctly?*

A No, not unless that's the type of pencil which is most comfortable. A choice of widths and lengths—short, long, wide, narrow—will help him decide what feels right for him. Offer him different kinds of pens, pencils, markers, crayons, sponge paint, and finger paint, as well as all kinds of papers and backgrounds.

Q *Will it hurt my daughter that she doesn't know how to read before she starts kindergarten?*

A No. Your daughter doesn't need to know how to read. As a kindergarten teacher, I always hoped the children who walked into my classroom were looking forward to school and had parents who provided a safe, loving, nurturing environment. This is what gives a child a true head start.

Q *Our daughter is five. How long in advance should we start preparing her for kindergarten?*

You have already started to prepare your daughter. How you've talked about children carrying their lunch boxes, what you've said about your own school experiences, and how you approached kindergarten registration have already helped her shape an opinion of school.

More targeted preparation begins about a month before school opens, perhaps around the same time ads for school supplies fall out of the Sunday newspaper. This will be a good time to include your daughter in buying decisions regarding a backpack, new shoes, and anything else included on the supply list mailed from your school. Listen carefully as your daughter shares her feelings about schedule changes and new friends.

Avoid the pitfall of making kindergarten your only topic. School should be one item on the agenda, but not the only one. Continue to support your child's play times with neighborhood friends and her out-of-school activities. Some children need a greater sense of continuity than others, but all new students need reassurance that familiar parts of life will continue, even though there is a major change coming.

Q My daughter doesn't want to pray by herself but wants me to pray for her. Should I?

A Yes. Support her prayer life by praying with and for your daughter. She has the opportunity to observe how, when, where and for what you pray.

Your daughter will use many kinds of prayer as she grows up. Right now she likes you to pray aloud for her. She might also pray silently, even though you might not see this happen.

God will listen to prayer, whether the words come from you or your daughter. Jesus reminds us, "I will do whatever you ask in my name, so that the Son may bring glory to the Father" (John 14:13).

Chapter Three

Early School-Age

FIVE TO SEVEN YEARS OLD

- "Packaged" parties easy
- Pre-party checklist
- Computer deprivation?
- "Real" restaurant
- Suppertime disaster
- Proving giftedness
- Too sensitive
- Bedtime stalling
- "Clean" room
- Hot lunch
- Fibs
- Won't eat at school
- Death
- Shooting

- Fine motor control
- Control television
- Reading—what age?
- Doesn't like reading
- Harsh realities
- School adjustment
- Wake
- Put away "stuff"
- Boring books
- Phoning parent at work
- Overhearing conversations
- Birthday greed
- Hesitant talker

Q Are "packaged" birthday parties as easy as they look?

A Yes, a "boxed" party at a local business has some real advantages. You don't stay up the night before cleaning the house and inflating balloons. Afterwards you don't have to clean up wrapping paper and cake crumbs. However, "packaged parties" almost always cost more than home parties.

Before you put down a deposit on a packaged party, list party expectations for you and your child. Plan an appropriate budget. Then determine if a party package will meet your goals.

A birthday party should help your child have a memorable time with friends or family. This can be done with your child across a kitchen table or in a children's gym crowded with friends.

🍂 🍂 🍂 🍂 🍂 🍂 🍂

Q Is it polite to check out in advance the place where my daughter wants to have her birthday party?

A I'm not an expert on etiquette, but I think a pre-party visit is essential. Here is a list of questions to take along:
• Will the activities match my child? (As the manager describes the activities, picture your child doing the games. Would your child have fun? Or, are the activities too babyish or too advanced?)

• What times are least crowded? (If the restaurant is packed with regular customers at usual "party times," this detracts from a "party" atmosphere.)

• How is the cost determined? (Know your own budget. Then ask appropriate questions. Are you charged for all children who are invited or only those who actually attend? Is there a minimum fee? Can you bring your own cake to reduce costs or purchase game tokens at a discounted rate, etc.? Is there an extra cost for additional adults? Also find out what party favors are provided for each guest. If large take-home bags are not included, consider bringing your own. It helps to have a personalized bag for each child in which to catch the items that seem to fall off children at parties—hair bows, glasses, mittens—as well as the prizes and game tickets they collect at the event.)

• Can you observe a party in progress? (This is the best way to determine whether or not the party and place will be appropriate for your birthday child.)

• What does the management provide to help your child feel special? (Helping your child feel special should be a major goal of any party, whether at home or elsewhere.)

• What kinds of supervision does the management provide? (Do you run the party or is that done by an experienced staff person? What measures are taken to keep guests and personal possessions safe?)

🍎 🍎 🍎 🍎 🍎 🍎 🍎

Q *I can't afford a computer. Will my kids be behind at school?*

A Children need security, love, appropriate limits, and a safe and healthy environment. They also need the chance to play with friends, go places, learn to listen, talk, share, win, and lose. A computer is not a "must."

But a computer can help a child build self-confidence, strengthen and accelerate specific skills, and increase, to a certain degree, hand/eye coordination. A computer can be one avenue to certain kinds of growth.

❦ ❦ ❦ ❦ ❦ ❦ ❦

Q *I like to use real silverware and order from a menu, but how can I get our children to behave in a restaurant?*

A At home, role-play "eating out." Set up a fancy table. Use folded cloth napkins, salad forks, dinner forks, and non-plastic glasses. Model good table manners. You or a child might even want to "play" at being the server.

When your children are ready to eat out, choose a restaurant with quick, attentive service. Select carefully: some restaurants are more oriented toward family dining than others. Ask to be seated where the children see a lot of action. Request a booster chair if necessary, so your child can feel physically comfortable. Sit next to the child who will need the most help cutting food.

Order quickly; waiting is difficult for children. Play verbal games appropriate for your children's ages. Also visit the bathroom to wash hands.

Positively reinforce good behavior throughout the meal ("You asked for more water very politely," etc.). Show your children how much you enjoy the experience. Help them understand that the point of good manners is to help everyone enjoy being together.

Remember two things:

1. Have developmentally appropriate expectations. If you want to enjoy a long, leisurely meal, consider getting a baby-sitter to stay with young children while you go out.

2. Consistent use of good table manners is a gradual learning process.

Q *Our suppertime is a noisy disaster. We barely sit down and the children leave. Is it even possible to have the nice mealtime I remember as a child?*

A Yes. It is possible to have lively conversation and children who want to stay around to talk and listen. However, it is most likely to happen if:

• "Let's improve mealtime" is a goal for the entire family.

• The television, stereo, or game system is turned off during the supper hour.

• No one accepts phone calls during mealtime.

If you want to change the tone of your mealtime, begin by discussing expectations. This is important because your children might be perfectly happy with a short, haphazard meal broken up by repeated phone calls. Ask everyone the same question, "What is a good suppertime?" Discuss the answers.

Then consider what will work for your family at this time of year and at this time of life. Next use your new ideas for a week or two. When the predetermined time ends, talk about your experiment.

Family-living specialists indicate that families need certain touch points, or specific times when people of all ages can talk freely with one another. The dinner hour is a perfect time for this to happen.

🍎 🍎 🍎 🍎 🍎 🍎 🍎

Q *How can I prove to the school district that my daughter is gifted and should start kindergarten early?*

A Private testing can be done at your expense. Simply contact your local school and ask for the names of certified school psychologists who also have private clients.

I was double promoted. As a teacher, I have recommended advanced placement for students in several situations. Obviously, I am not against this kind of action in rare instances.

However, in the majority of cases, bright students can be challenged in a classroom where the teacher is aware of the student's skills and abilities and desires to meet the needs of all individuals. Teachers have an immense amount of support, enrichment, and advancement opportunities to offer students today. Such vast resources were not available years ago when I "skipped."

I am concerned about your question. Often, when parents want to "prove" advanced placement, the focus of testing becomes acceleration, not learning more about the child so the needs can be met more effectively.

Have your child tested only if you want to identify ways to most effectively meet her needs next year and beyond. Use the test results as a learning aid for you. I cannot recommend testing alone as a placement tool for your preschooler.

❧ ❧ ❧ ❧ ❧ ❧ ❧

Q My son was grumpy all day because his favorite shirt was in the wash. I think he's too sensitive about little things, but I don't know what to do.

A Children are no different from adults: feelings about our appearance can influence our feelings about everything.

Some children worry more, others worry less about the little things of life. There are a variety of theories that attempt to explain such individual tendencies, but your son's behavior appears normal. After all, even parents occasionally have a bad hair day.

❦ ❦ ❦ ❦ ❦ ❦ ❦

Q My kids stall at bedtime. Then there's only time for a fast kiss before "lights out." What should I do?

A Stalling, in some form or another, is part of bedtime. Build stalling time into your nightly routine.

A good way to examine what happens at bedtime is to jot down what happens tonight. Then, after the children are in bed, write down what you'd like to happen: simply write your "lights out" time at the top of the page, and then plan backward. Compare the pages, and you'll easily identify where the time goes.

First, eliminate or reschedule activities that have a built-in potential for conflict. For example, if you and your child tend to have lengthy discussions about what he's wearing to school the next day, change your pattern. Talk about that immediately after supper or, better yet, let him make his own choice. If the dog running between rooms tends to distract children, remove the family pet from the area. That will prevent you from hearing, "I need to tell Skippy 'Good night' one last time."

Second, add five to ten minutes of free time to help children wind down naturally. This allows for the inevitable calling back and forth between brother and sister, looking for a lost shoe, and other excuses. But there's a difference to this approach from the usual stalling routine: you plan for this up front.

Some parents set a timer for fifteen or twenty minutes. During that time, children can be expected to brush teeth and finish up other routines before lights are turned out. Children will hurry if the first one done gets extra time with you.

❧ ❧ ❧ ❧ ❧ ❧ ❧

Q My daughter tells me her room is clean when it's still a mess. What can I do?

A There are four actions you can take to remove potential sources of conflict:

• Make the room easy for a child to manage. Remove unnecessary clutter. Rearrange the room if the bed is against the wall and hard to make. Replace layers of blankets and a decorative bedspread with a comforter that can also serve as a bedspread. Make sure she has accessible storage and a variety of storage bins, a low closet rod and plenty of hangers and pegs, and her own laundry and waste baskets.

• Clarify expectations. Your definition of a "clean room" might be totally different from your daughter's definition. She might think a clean room is jamming dirty clothes in the closet. You might think a room is clean when the shelves are dusted and clothes are neatly folded in drawers or hung in the closet. Negotiate an acceptable definition of a "clean room."

• Teach the job. Does your daughter know how to fold jeans to fit into a drawer or clean a mirror so it doesn't have streaks? Review with your daughter each of the job skills necessary to have a clean room. Then have patience as she learns.

• Make sure jobs are developmentally appropriate. Your daughter may not know how to lift a mattress to put on a fitted sheet without ripping the corner. Or her arms might not be long enough to safely reach dust on the top shelf. Assist as needed.

❧ ❧ ❧ ❧ ❧ ❧ ❧

Q The menus sound very good, but I can't get my first grader to eat a hot lunch in the school cafeteria.

Standing in a line, making some quick food choices you might not even be able to see if you're seven years old, and balancing a heavy tray are all part of eating a school lunch. It might be one of these aspects—and not the food at all—that keeps your child from buying lunch. Also, a sandwich packed at home by Mom might be a nice "security blanket" for a child surrounded by older kids in a busy, noisy cafeteria.

I suggest you and your child continue to pack a nutritious lunch and not worry about school food.

🍎 🍎 🍎 🍎 🍎 🍎 🍎

Q *My daughter has gotten into a habit of telling little fibs. She knows she's doing it and wants to stop. How can I help?*

A It's great that she wants to break a bad habit. Develop a code or signal, so that when your daughter begins to tell a lie, you can snap your finger or click your tongue to indicate she needs to catch herself. Once she's aware of the problem, she can learn to stop the fibbing before it happens.

🍎 🍎 🍎 🍎 🍎 🍎 🍎

Q *My son started full-day kindergarten. Every day for the first two weeks, he's brought home an almost-full lunch box.*

A Check with his teacher or the cafeteria supervisor. If they say everything is fine, just give the situation a little time.

• Pack small amounts. A young child doesn't need a banquet. Sometimes parents think, "My poor child will starve if I don't load the lunch box." That's not true.

• Let your child choose what he takes. If you wish, offer snack-type items that might even stimulate his friends to say, "Wow! Is that neat. You get peanut butter cups." Return to more solid nutrition once your child starts eating.

• Look beyond two pieces of bread. Consider cheese cubes on little plastic swords (like the ones adults use at parties), a salami stick, frozen pudding, etc. Many children don't like sandwiches unless they come from a local fast-food restaurant.

• Help him look beyond his own lunch box. Make a batch of cookies together so he can take a whole bag to share with his friends, for example.

• Eat lunch at school with him. Plan it casually, and don't dwell on the lunch topic. Some schools set aside one day a month for parents and grandparents to eat with children, so find out how your school handles this.

• Talk with your child. Believe him if he says, "I'm just not that hungry."

• Focus on variety. Plan small amounts of four or five different foods, so if one food doesn't seem appealing, he still has other choices. Begin with half a sandwich, for example, instead of always packing a whole sandwich.

• Don't push. He will survive this, and so will you.

❧ ❧ ❧ ❧ ❧ ❧ ❧

Q When my son asks about his grandfather's death, how much detail should I go into?

A Answer his questions truthfully with as much detail as you feel will help him understand. Take cues from your son. For example, if your son is young, you might say, "Grandpa had a heart attack. That means his heart stopped beating." An older child might ask additional questions about the life-saving methods medical personnel attempted or the technology that was used.

In situations about death, spirituality, sexuality, and other potentially "deep" subjects, let your child ask the questions, if at all possible. Watch his verbal and nonverbal clues to be sure you've answered his question. If your child doesn't appear to understand your answer, it's not necessarily because you've done a poor job of explaining. Sometimes, children don't know exactly how to phrase questions. Then, we simply need to explain using a different approach at a later date.

❦ ❦ ❦ ❦ ❦ ❦ ❦

Q Is it harmful for my son to pretend to shoot? He even turns a table fork or baseball bat into a gun.

A Generations of children have played superheroes. Past experience indicates that such pretend play in limited, isolated situations is not, in itself, harmful.

However, in the past, what we read in newspapers didn't happen in our backyards. Daily violence didn't come into our homes through television murders, video-game shootings, and gruesome newspaper accounts of domestic abuse. Children today are exposed to real-life violence in many different ways. Consistent play using violent themes can negatively influence behavior.

A child who regularly acts in physically aggressive ways during play may begin to adopt those kinds of actions in other situations. Just ask any parent whose child has dressed in a pirate or lion costume: soon the child doesn't just wear the clothes but acts the part. Children today are so repeatedly exposed to violence, the lines between fact and fiction can easily become blurred.

Make sure your son has enough opportunity to work out feelings with a backyard tether ball, sand box, or wheeled toy.

Redirect play that remains focused on a single "wild" theme every day. Also introduce potential role models who express their feelings in words and appropriate actions, exhibit caring and compassion, and use positive problem-solving methods.

🍎 🍎 🍎 🍎 🍎 🍎 🍎

Q The kindergarten teacher says my son "has poor fine motor control. Have him string beads." My son is all-boy. He will not like stringing beads! What else can he do?

A It's great the teacher suggested an action-oriented activity instead of having your son sit down with a pencil and paper. You'll want to give him a lot of or many chances to use the small muscles in his hands. That's what the teacher means by fine motor control. Try these things:

• Help him learn to fold paper airplanes. Check out some library books that show various kinds of planes. Five and six year olds are just getting into paper-folding.

• Provide a lot of building and construction toys: Legos, American Bricks, Tinker Toys, or anything that requires him to really work those small muscles.

• Ask him to sort nails, screws, nuts, and bolts in the tool box.

• Keep a shoebox filled with salt in the kitchen. While you're preparing food, he can trace letters, make pictures, or race small toy cars in the salt with his fingers.

• Help him learn to zip his own coat, to button, and to snap. Don't force him to tie shoes yet; that's a complicated skill.

• Do jigsaw puzzles together. They're terrific for small muscles.

• Encourage your child to use your computer or a hand-held video game. Most children like the excuse to type on a keyboard or use a joystick, and these activities also offer practice in small motor coordination.

❧ ❧ ❧ ❧ ❧ ❧ ❧

Q *I think an electronic device that blocks out bad programs is an artificial way to solve the television problem. Children should be guided by God's commandment on honoring parents. Do you have a comment?*

A There are many ways to tame the tube. The end results of any viewing-choice system should be to ensure that TV has a proper place (if desired) in the family life.

Different strategies will work for different families at different times. Use of a blocking device does not necessarily imply that the children in this family disobey the commandment any more than your children or mine. Your neighbor might appreciate electronic aids while you might close the doors of an entertainment center to limit TV use. You are both dealing with a potential problem, but using a different solution.

❧ ❧ ❧ ❧ ❧ ❧ ❧

Q *By what age should my son know how to read?*

A There is no one specific age at which all needed skills and abilities come together for everyone. In the United States, educators have decided that most children should learn to read in first grade. However, this type of standard does not take into account the tremendous range of individual differences. In other countries, there is much greater flexibility with the reading time line.

🍎 🍎 🍎 🍎 🍎 🍎 🍎

Q *My second grader doesn't enjoy reading. I've checked often with the teachers, and she reads very well. But at home, she never chooses, on her own, to read a book.*

My husband and I read a lot. We've taken her to the library since she was little. But she still doesn't enjoy reading. I'm disappointed. Is there anything else I can do?

A You already are doing a lot. You've checked on her progress at school. You and your husband are providing good models of the importance and joy of reading. You have given your daughter opportunities to read, and I assume you've had her eyes checked on a regular basis. You have done a wonderful job.

As a seven or eight year old, your daughter has many options to fill her free time. She might play with dolls, building blocks, or neighborhood friends. All are good and developmentally appropriate activities.

We, on the other hand, might savor sitting down to read during our brief leisure time. It might not seem right that a child doesn't want to use time in the way we would. But there's the key difference. Your child is her own person. Even the "almost perfect" parent sometimes finds it hard to accept that individuality, especially when we want so much to share a certain love and interest with our child.

Your daughter has many wonderful years ahead. Some of that time might be filled with the joy of reading. She can build on the wonderful basics you are providing.

🍎 🍎 🍎 🍎 🍎 🍎 🍎

Q *When my six year old asked if people and dogs were killed in some recent flooding, I didn't know how to answer his question.*

A Answer your child's questions honestly. Children need to hear the truth.

Also answer questions immediately. That's important because your son can imagine a scenario far worse than what actually happened.

Your child's understanding of a disaster or tragedy will be shaped by his developmental level. That means he probably can't comprehend the specifics of the flooding, a tornado, or the causes of a wildfire, but answer his questions as clearly as possible. He can ask for more information when he's ready for a more complicated response.

🍎 🍎 🍎 🍎 🍎 🍎 🍎

Q *My five year old had a terrible time adjusting to kindergarten. Does that mean she'll have trouble adjusting to first grade?*

A No. Most kindergarten teachers help students begin this transition during the last weeks of the school year.

Kindergartners often recognize their future teachers from seeing them in the hallways. Also, many primary grades work together on various experiences during the year, so your daughter has probably visited the first grade to perform a puppet show or listen to first graders read. When the classrooms are in the same school, most kindergarten teachers will make sure the students meet potential teachers, sit at the first grade tables, and generally get a feel of the new rooms.

When first graders will be in a different school, most districts try to ensure a good transition. Some host "open houses" before the first day; others invite first graders and parents to visit rooms during registration; others set up individual appointments for students and teachers to visit briefly.

Share your concern with your daughter's kindergarten teacher, but avoid communicating to your child, "I think you're going to have trouble getting used to first grade."

Do just what you did before your child started kindergarten: Emphasize the positive, avoid drawing a lot of attention to the issue, and expect her to handle the situation very well. She will be one year older. She has already managed the basic adjustment to school. She is moving to first grade from a position of strength.

Q How do I decide if I should take my daughter to a wake?

A Ask yourself, "How would she benefit?"

Many experts feel that older children who participate in rituals related to death learn naturally about life cycles, observe the normal grieving process, and have the opportunity to ask questions about death and dying.

These general benefits must always be applied to the specific situation and developmental level of the child. If you feel your child can grow from the experience, discuss the option with her and then make a decision.

Q How can I get my son to put away his stuff after school?

A   Here is a step-by-step plan:
1. Determine what will be an acceptable solution to you. Decide what you want to happen with his school things.

2. Review with your son what has been happening. Go together to look at the book bag that was dropped in the hall or the gym shoes that were left at the front door. This will clearly illustrate the problem.

3. Share concerns and goals. Ask for your child's input. Offer your support, as needed. For example, you might say, "Your lunch box needs to be emptied out in the kitchen before supper. How can I help you make that happen?"

4. Propose a plan. You might say, "Let me show you today how to spend less than one minute cleaning out your lunch box. Tomorrow, you can do it. Throw away the leftover food and wrappings that were in your lunch box. If you used a Thermos, rinse it out with hot water. Leave it open to dry. Use a damp paper towel to wipe the lunch box. Then set everything here on the counter."

5. Try the plan for about a week. Then evaluate. If this has not worked, try another approach. The bottom line is that your child should accept some responsibility for his school equipment.

🍎 🍎 🍎 🍎 🍎 🍎 🍎

Q   *My seven year old is supposed to read boring books aloud every night, and he hates it.*

A   Get approval from his teacher to have your son dictate a story to you each night. You can write down what he says, and read it back together. Occasionally, cut the writing paper into different shapes to trigger some creative thinking.

Then post your daily story on the refrigerator or in his bedroom. In this way, he'll be surrounded by written language that is important to him.

You might also encourage him to dictate a letter to a cousin or a grandparent. When your child receives a letter in return, he'll get a little extra reading practice, because receiving mail is one certain way to encourage even reluctant readers to read.

Also ask the teacher to either suggest "non-boring" books or get permission for your son to read books or magazines that he has chosen.

🍎 🍎 🍎 🍎 🍎 🍎 🍎

Q I am starting a new job. Should I tell my children where they can reach me at work, or will they want to call me all the time?

A It's important your children know they can contact you if necessary. Give them your office number (and your extension if needed), emergency numbers, and the number of at least one other adult they could call.

Take two actions to help your children distinguish between emergencies and questions:

1. Play "What if?" Talk through some problem situations. Ask your children to help you think up questions like these:

• "What if you turn on the microwave, and the microwave won't work?"

• "What if someone comes to the door and insists they have fresh flowers that will wilt if they are left outside?"

• "What if there's a thunderstorm, and the electricity goes out?"

2. Post a short list next to the phone that will be quick and easy to read in a real emergency:

• If there's a fire, call . . .

• If anyone is hurt, call . . .

• If you have a question that needs to be answered now, call

Grandma at . . .

• If you aren't sure what to do about something, call . . .

• If you have a question or message that can wait until I get home, write it here . . .

Children learn through experience, growing maturity, and teaching opportunities like these to distinguish between real emergencies and everyday situations.

While your children are in school, they will be limited by school rules to making only emergency calls, so I doubt you will hear from them often. Before starting this job, make sure the school office has your new work number and current emergency numbers.

Also, talk with anyone whom you suggest your children can call if they have questions. Neighbors and relatives are usually glad to help, but it's important to alert them in advance to the new role you are asking them to assume.

❧ ❧ ❧ ❧ ❧ ❧ ❧

Q *When driving a car full of children, is it all right to listen to what they are saying and participate in their conversation?*

A Unless the children are whispering, it's hard to keep something secret in the small space of a car. Children know that a driver would naturally overhear much of what is spoken in a normal tone of voice. Sometimes children say things in such a setting simply because they want us to hear.

Participate in a discussion only if you're invited. It's appropriate to respond if asked, "What do you think?" or "Can we do that?" (Obviously, the children know you've already heard what they've said.)

Discussing personal issues should take place, whenever possible, in the privacy of the home or when alone in the car with your child.

❦ ❦ ❦ ❦ ❦ ❦ ❦

Q *It's two months before my son's birthday, but he's already made a list of presents. How can I keep him from being greedy but not ruin the specialness of a birthday?*

A You expressed very clearly the dilemma of helping a child balance dreams and reality. Use a gentle approach to help your child prioritize and realistically anticipate. For example, you might say, "Wow, that's a really long wish list. Perhaps we can get you several of those things. Please mark the ones you want most."

❦ ❦ ❦ ❦ ❦ ❦ ❦

Q *My third grader is hesitant to speak in front of the class. How can I help her?*

A Experience and positive reinforcement will be most helpful. Third grade is often the first time children are asked to make a presentation in front of the class. Some students get extremely nervous, so your child is not alone in her feelings.

Your daughter might want to substitute some transition activities as she adjusts to speaking in public. For example, she might want to tape record a description of her social studies project. Talking into a microphone is much easier than talking in front of other third graders. Or, your daughter might use school equipment to video tape a book report.

At this point, just help her cope with it so she gradually feels more comfortable. Some children (like some adults) simply don't enjoy public speaking.

Assure your daughter her feelings are normal. Talk about some times when you were a bit nervous about speaking. Share the stress-reduction techniques that worked for you. Then give your daughter support and encouragement.

Tweenagers

EIGHT TO TWELVE YEARS OLD

* No time to play
* Organizing homework
* Baseball cards
* Kids "turning out"?
* Family devotions
* Television news
* Murder scare
* Quit reading program?
* Scary dream
* Bedtime stories
* Hanging out at mall
* Creative birthday gifts
* Backpack argument
* Older child privileges
* Learning disability

* Private phone line
* Threats to run away
* Major move
* Teen at age eleven
* Loner
* Bedtime stalling
* Moping around
* Lost election
* Older adoption
* Baby-sitting
* Odd clothes
* Rereading same books
* Chores vs. homework
* Boys on the phone

Q My daughter gets so much homework in fifth grade she doesn't have time to play after school.

A Homework should not consume the whole evening, night after night. For one week, you and your child should keep track of time—in five-minute segments—from the moment your child gets home until she goes to bed. Separate time spent doing homework from time watching television, practicing a music lesson, or participating in after-school activities. Record how much time is actually spent on each subject every night for the five days.

Add up your figures at the end of the week. If you feel the amount of time spent in homework was excessive, make an appointment with your child's teacher. Take your chart to the conference. The teacher might not realize the assignments are taking students so long to complete and will appreciate your input.

❦ ❦ ❦ ❦ ❦ ❦ ❦

Q How can I help my fourth grader organize her homework?

A One of the major tasks of fourth grade is learning how to organize, so your question is very appropriate.

Most fourth-grade teachers give very specific suggestions on how to organize a folder and notebook. Ask your child to show you how school materials are organized in the classroom, so you can support the procedures set by the teacher.

Ask your daughter to write down all assignments before she leaves the classroom. A small assignment book with a pencil attached might help her keep track of her work. Review the homework list after school. Encourage your daughter to check off every assignment as she works through the list each night.

Children sometimes feel organization is a one-time task. If your daughter learns that organization is a continual process for which she is responsible, she will have discovered an important key to a successful school career.

❦ ❦ ❦ ❦ ❦ ❦ ❦

Q How can I stop my nine year old from wasting all his time and some of his money on baseball cards?

A I wouldn't stop him. Sports cards offer the potential for learning about statistics, strategy, and personalities and can help children develop a lifelong interest in sports. If the cards become more than a seasonal interest, as is true for many "tweenage" boys, he might develop a collection that's worth money. And one of the greatest benefits is that your son won't need to spend money to get more cards—he can just trade.

❦ ❦ ❦ ❦ ❦ ❦ ❦

Q What are signs that my children are turning out all right?

A Exterior reflections of growth, including participation in sports, music, or drama; peer activities; health records; and adult feedback can indicate healthy child development.

Our own "gut level" perception, coupled with information from any sound parenting book like this, is another helpful means of assessment. After all, we know our children so well: we know what motivates them, excites them, and scares them; we've heard their dreams and nightmares. When we combine our perceptions with more objective measures like report-card grades, we probably have a fairly accurate view of how our children are developing.

However, there's no guarantee your children or mine will "turn out." Our children will make many judgments and choices which will shape their lives. As parents, we can simply do our best and count on God's faithfulness.

❧ ❧ ❧ ❧ ❧ ❧ ❧

Q Are boys aged eight and eleven too old for family devotions?

A No, but it can be a challenge to find materials that match the increasingly varied interests of children during the preteen years. And because "tweenagers" like to show they are growing up, changing the pattern of family devotions might be one way to acknowledge this new stage in life. Fortunately, there isn't a single "right" way to spend time with God.

Discuss the issue with your sons. Then offer various options. Instead of using a traditional format, you might have a longer family prayer at mealtime. Or, because children begin to develop areas of special interest during these years, have bedtime devotions individually with each boy. Your oldest son might like to begin a program to read through the Bible in three years, especially if a cousin or grandparent is also following the same program. You might shorten family devotions and include some time for individual Bible reading. Encourage your sons to help design a devotional plan that meets their needs.

❧ ❧ ❧ ❧ ❧ ❧ ❧

Q I have always watched the television news after supper. Now that the kids understand the meaning of the news stories (like child abuse, murder, rape), I don't think they should be exposed to the graphic violence. But I don't want to give up watching the news.

A Before you focus on the problems of TV, ask yourself, "What do I want from this time segment of the evening?"

Some parents feel that viewing television news with their children triggers meaningful conversation. If there's a potential to teach your children through the nightly news, mute or skip the commercials and discuss topics during the breaks.

We can't shield our children forever from the harsh realities of life. But we can be our children's best television guide. If you decide the content of television news is presented in ways inappropriate for prime-time family viewing, turn it off. Contact your local station and share your feelings.

Discuss the issue with your children. Let them see how you identify a problem, consider options, and make a decision.

If you do turn the TV off after dinner, you still have ways to keep up with the latest news. Consider reading the newspaper, watching a later newscast, videotaping the after-dinner news segment to view later, or listening to an all-news station on the radio.

※ ※ ※ ※ ※ ※ ※

Q *After a murder that made headlines, my nine year old asked a lot of questions. She wanted to know, "Where did they find the gun?" and "How did it happen?" so I gave her the newspaper with the story. It's too late now, but I wonder if that was the right thing to do.*

A Children need three things in this kind of situation:

1. Information. The facts should be geared to their level of understanding. Your nine year old was probably able to get factual answers from what she read in the newspaper.

2. Interpretation. We often need to fill in the details or help our children process the information. For example, if your nine year

old read, "Two suspects have been taken into custody," you could ask her to explain in her own words what that means.

3. Reassurance. Our children need to be reminded of the many ways in which we try to protect them.

❧ ❧ ❧ ❧ ❧ ❧ ❧

My nine year old signed up for a library reading program, but now he doesn't want to continue. Should I force him to read the books he's supposed to read?

If signing up for the program was initially his choice and not yours, listen to why he changed his mind. If he only says, "I just don't want to," find out what activity he intends to substitute to fill that time. Also, ask how he intends to keep up reading skills without the program.

If you forced him to sign up for the program in the first place, share your original goal for him. As a preadolescent, he can make leisure-time choices, so encourage him to participate in making the next decision.

Also, help your son view this incident as an opportunity to weigh both sides of an issue and then make a wise choice. He might even want to write points related to "I should quit" and "I should continue." This type of practice in decision-making can be valuable to a nine year old.

❧ ❧ ❧ ❧ ❧ ❧ ❧

We didn't have time to talk when my nine year old mentioned a scary dream she had. Would it be good to bring up the subject or would that remind her about something that was scary?

A Without making it a big deal, give her the opportunity to talk about the dream. Try to communicate these elements:
1. Affirm her talking to you.
2. It's not unusual to remember some dreams.
3. Dreams do not always turn into reality.

A sample script might read, "If you'd like to talk about that scary dream again, I'd be glad to listen. I know we didn't have time to talk when you mentioned it. I've had scary dreams, too, and I know it's unsettling. Isn't it good to know that what we remember from our dreams doesn't always happen?"

This approach will leave the door open for her to talk with you, but it doesn't draw exceptional attention to her concern.

❧ ❧ ❧ ❧ ❧ ❧ ❧

Q *My nine year old goofs off when I try to read a bedtime story to him and the younger kids. Reading has always been a nice way to end the day, but it's becoming a hassle.*

A Reading at bedtime is an excellent way to settle down children and have a few minutes of peace for us, too. Perhaps now would be a good time to continue a great tradition in new ways.

If you want to continue reading with all your children together, you'll need to physically and mentally involve your older son. You might read aloud alternate paragraphs with your nine year old, for example.

Or, you might want to start a separate reading time with your oldest. What you'll probably notice is that not only will the kind of books he chooses be too advanced for the younger children, but the kinds of discussions you have before or after reading will be more appropriate for his age.

A book is simply a starting point. As the author of many children's books, I visualize that the adult and child who are reading the book will continue talking after finishing the last page. I know that the benefit might not be in the book, but in the process of reading and sharing that happens between the pages.

This concept of reading as a launch point for communication will be increasingly important as your son grows older. Often, reading aloud can help build an atmosphere that leads to discussing and answering questions. And that's something your oldest child will continue to appreciate.

❦ ❦ ❦ ❦ ❦ ❦ ❦

Q *Isn't my ten year old too young to be dropped off at the mall "just to walk around" with friends?*

A Yes. Ten year olds need some independence and an opportunity to be alone with friends. However, hanging out in the basement or on a front porch is a far more appropriate place than a mall.

You can, however, gradually help your daughter handle herself alone in public places. For example, you might want to take her and her friends to a movie. You might sit in one section of the theater while the girls (and with ten year olds the group will be all female) settle into a different row. Make arrangements to meet after the show at the concession stand. This kind of observation from a distance allows your daughter a sense of freedom and gives you the opportunity to observe how she handles the situation.

When your daughter is twelve or thirteen and she wants to hang out at the mall with friends, plan the trip to coincide with your own shopping. Meet at a designated place every half hour. Gradually decrease the amount of supervision.

But in any of these situations, it's tough to set an ideal age at which something might occur. Your own personal parenting style and your daughter's general level of maturity, peer group, and past experiences will be more important than age guidelines.

$ $ $ $ $ $ $

Q *My nephew is a ten year old who has everything. Do you have any ideas of what I can buy for his birthday?*

A Consider these gifts:
• Something to read. A book is a gift he'll open again and again. Preteen boys are often fans of a specific fiction series, or they enjoy reading about a certain sport or type of collectible.
• A gift certificate to a sports shop, arcade, music store, video store, or other specialty store.
• Tickets to a game, concert, or event. Check with his parents for available dates before you get the tickets. You might get a ticket for both of you and a friend he'd like to invite.

$ $ $ $ $ $ $

Q *Is it worth a big fight to force my son to use a perfectly good back-pack that he says isn't "in"?*

A Probably not, but it's really your call. As parents, we sometimes "major in the minors" or put too much energy and emphasis on things that aren't that important. This could be one of those situations, so it's good you're thinking about a realistic response.

As children grow older, they have a growing desire to be part of the group. Now might be an excellent time to talk about peer pressure.

If your son really wants a different backpack, help him put together a plan for him to earn at least some of the money to buy the replacement. For example, he might be hired to clean the garage, paint a fence, etc.

Also, discuss ways to recycle the "perfectly good backpack." Perhaps he could use it as a gear bag for sports, to store bulky items in the closet, etc.

🐦 🐦 🐦 🐦 🐦 🐦 🐦

Q *What do you think of giving a ten year old privileges that her younger brother and sister don't get, just because she's the oldest?*

A All children should learn that both privileges and responsibilities come with age. It's developmentally appropriate that a ten year old could go to bed fifteen minutes later than an eight year old. A ten year old also could learn how to fold laundry; that might not be expected of an eight year old.

🐦 🐦 🐦 🐦 🐦 🐦 🐦

Q *Our ten-year-old son was just diagnosed with a learning disability. How could the teachers have missed it all these years?*

A School psychologists typically receive a lot of referrals for testing around fourth grade. That's because some problems are not clearly obvious in the early years. In addition, some children learn how to compensate for weaknesses during the early grades when teachers use "hands-on" instruction.

But around fourth grade, teaching strategies change. By this time, students should have developed independent work skills which allow them to perform self-directed learning. For example, not only is there a spelling test at the end of the week, as in third grade, but there is also a history report due at the end of the month and a science project due in two months. You can see that these kinds of assignments require your child to become more aggressive in guiding his own learning. At this time, problems that may have been there all along might suddenly be uncovered.

$$* * * * * * *$$

Q My eleven year old wants her own phone. Even though I think she's too young, it's frustrating to have her tie up the phone.

A Some parents purchase phones for their young adults as a means of self-preservation. That's understandable. But you can also view the issue of personal phone ownership as a discussion point for increased responsibility.

Some parents choose to give their child a phone, but the child pays the monthly bills. Other parents feel preteens should be just as responsible as any other family member in sensitive phone use. The phone(s) in these homes are shared by everyone.

Other parents permit children to have phones when they can pay all the costs: installation, purchase price, and continuing fees. For this option to work, your daughter will need a continuing source of income (money earned from lawn-care jobs, baby-sitting, etc.).

Your daughter is old enough to think about the problem and offer some solutions. Discuss options with her, and then make a thoughtful decision.

❦ ❦ ❦ ❦ ❦ ❦ ❦

Q When my eleven year old gets really mad, she'll yell, "I'll just run away," and I say, "Go ahead." I worry that someday she'll do just that.

A Tweenagers, whose bodies are changing before their eyes and who face swirling emotions every day, want to feel that they control their feelings. They also want parents to recognize that they have reached this new stage of development.

Getting into a long, drawn-out argument merely trades feelings; it just doesn't work. Keep your conversation short and to the point. Listen carefully to her comments. You can help your daughter learn to talk about her feelings when you:

1. Acknowledge her feelings. Let her know you are listening. You might say, "It sounds like you're upset."

2. Find out why your daughter feels this way. Simply ask, "What happened?" This will encourage her to think about and talk through the incident so she can understand her own reaction.

❦ ❦ ❦ ❦ ❦ ❦ ❦

Q How can I help my daughter adjust to a major move?

A A move can be totally overwhelming for parents and children. Be especially kind to yourself during this time of transition. To maximize benefits and minimize trauma for your daughter:

1. Involve her in the preparation. If she can't accompany you on a pre-move visit to the new city, bring back pictures of where you'll be living, some child-oriented sites in the new location (zoo,

children's museum, etc.), and a photo of the school or day care center she'll attend.

2. Match the preparation time to your child. Some children adjust more easily if they are aware of many details far in advance; others prefer knowing very little and then having that information just prior to the event. Apply your personal knowledge of your child to this and all other aspects of the move.

3. Allow your child to keep special things with her until the last moment. Then take that box of items in the car or on the plane with you. Tangible, familiar objects can become very important to a child when all other supports have changed.

4. During the whole process, encourage her to be honest with her emotions. Set aside time to listen, encourage, and talk. Empathize with her feelings, assuring her, "I'm going to miss my friends, too."

5. Once you have relocated, establish familiar routines as soon as possible. Also, arrange her personal space as soon as possible.

6. Immediately after the move, encourage your daughter to keep in touch with friends and relatives. These will be important personal connections.

🐞 🐞 🐞 🐞 🐞 🐞 🐞

Q *What's wrong? My daughter is acting like a teenager, but she's only eleven.*

A If you are observing mood swings, general discontent, or behavior that indicates, "I'm too cool for my family," everything appears normal. Right now, your daughter is probably going through hormonal changes. The average girl begins the growth spurt that is associated with puberty at the age of ten and a half.

Give your daughter an extra measure of support and encouragement; the behaviors you observe are probably outward signs of the tremendous internal changes she's experiencing.

❦ ❦ ❦ ❦ ❦ ❦ ❦

Q *My son wants to go with some teenagers to play some kind of game called paintball. Evidently, it's played outside, and kids try to find a flag before they are hit with a paintball. He says it's harmless, but I'm not sure.*

A There are many versions of paintball, but basically players run around with air guns from which they shoot pellets of water-based paint. Players wear safety goggles and sometimes padding for protection against the sting of the shots.

Paintball guns were initially used by foresters to mark trees to be cut down, and ranch hands to mark livestock during round-ups. Now, paintball is played indoors in special facilities as well as outside on farms and in fields.

According to sporting statistics, the game appears relatively safe. However, the real question is whether you and your son feel it's a good idea to go around shooting people.

❦ ❦ ❦ ❦ ❦ ❦ ❦

Q *I don't know how to stop my eleven year old from a new form of bedtime stalling. He will often come downstairs to ask questions and talk long after he should be asleep.*

A This is not unusual. Many preteens lie awake in bed before they fall asleep. There's a lot going on in their lives, and this is one of the few times they have quiet thinking time.

Simply listen to your son, reassure him, and send him back to bed.

But you can probably prevent this whole situation from happening. Ask your son to write down his problems and worries as they appear during the day. Then each night before bedtime, set aside time to talk. Follow through with this every single night, so your son can count on regular, private talking time. Also share your expectation. You might say, "I will talk with you each night, but when you go to bed, I expect you to stay in bed."

Give him a pad of paper and a pencil. Then, if he gets new ideas or concerns as he lies in bed, he can write them down and share them with you the following night.

❧ ❧ ❧ ❧ ❧ ❧ ❧

Q *My eleven-year-old daughter mopes around for stupid reasons: somebody didn't phone, or her jeans aren't right, or I won't let her stay over at somebody's house. How can I manage this mopey, whiny time?*

A First, avoid a deep discussion on "Why are you acting like this?" Such conversations tend to go in a circle and accomplish very little. However, there are actions you can take:

1. View the world from your daughter's perspective. Looking through adult eyes, the reasons for her behavior may seem unimportant. However, when we look through the eyes of a tweenager, eager to fit into the peer group, social glitches may appear major.

2. Help her look past herself. After a seemingly disastrous social experience, a tweenager may ask, "How can I ever go back to school?" or "If he talks to me, what can I say?" Encourage her to focus outward, toward others. Be alert for ways she can volunteer with friends in your church and community. Often, problems in a

small social group decrease in importance and intensity when they are put into a bigger life picture.

❧ ❧ ❧ ❧ ❧ ❧ ❧

Q *My daughter, who was always on student council in elementary school, lost the junior high election, because, she said, it was a "popularity contest." Should I talk to the principal about this?*

A Yes, although it would be better if your daughter talks to the principal.

Student council at this school may be set up differently than in her past school. Classroom teachers, the group sponsor, and the council members' job descriptions influence whether student council representatives are chosen on the basis of responsibility or popularity.

If student council members simply sell apples at school games and stand up at school assemblies, popularity wins.

If, on the other hand, student council members provide real school services (mentoring younger students, working in drug abuse awareness, etc.), representatives should be chosen for their ability to act responsibly. That would be emphasized during any "campaigning." Even the way a teacher introduces a vote in the classroom, "Vote for the person you feel best represents our school to the community," can influence election results.

What's important is that your daughter has a niche in the school. Encourage her to participate in music, sports, or other activities that can provide a social base and give her a sense of meaning.

❧ ❧ ❧ ❧ ❧ ❧ ❧

Q *We adopted older children. Is the statement true, "If you don't teach them young, you lose them?"*

A Young children need nurturing caregivers; patterns of relating and behaving are established early in life. However, even if early-childhood conditions are unknown or negative, these can sometimes be modified, or new patterns can be established.

Every stage of child development is important and requires active parenting. Although early-childhood experiences provide a foundation, effective nurturing at any age can make a positive difference.

❧ ❧ ❧ ❧ ❧ ❧ ❧

Q *At what age should my son start watching somebody other than his own siblings?*

A Children often begin baby-sitting around the age of eleven or twelve, but a child's age isn't the most important factor. Before baby-sitting, your son should reach a certain level of maturity. He should have good judgment and the ability to respond appropriately in various situations. He should also enjoy children.

If your child is interested in baby-sitting, ask why he wants to baby-sit. Then pose some "What if?" scenarios to help him think through real-life issues. This will also give you an opportunity to assess his readiness. For example, you might ask, "What will you do if someone rings the doorbell?" or "How will you respond if one of Cody's friends comes into the backyard to play?"

Also consider these factors:

• Would you or another adult be nearby if your child needed help?

  • How long will the parent be gone?
  • During what hours would he baby-sit?
  • What is the age of the child he would be watching?
  • How many children are involved?
  • Does your son already know the family?

Help your child develop a list of questions to ask parents before they leave: parents' return time, children's bedtimes, snack options for the children, any foods to avoid, emergency numbers, children's favorite activities, TV limitations, etc. Good questions will uncover the house rules as well as the expectations of the parents and the children.

I highly recommend that youth complete the Safe Sitter program (1500 N. Ritter Ave., Indianapolis, IN 46219) to gain skills and build confidence. Or, contact your local hospital, day-care association, or YMCA for available programs. Scouts often complete training to earn a child-care badge, so a Scout leader might have some suggestions. Or, ask your school nurse or administrator if your parent association can host a baby-sitting clinic.

❧ ❧ ❧ ❧ ❧ ❧ ❧

Q I can't understand why, all of a sudden, my twelve year old wants to buy the oddest looking clothes at resale shops.

A We know that our personal appearance tells something about us. Adolescents try to fit into the crowd or establish their uniqueness with outlandish haircuts, clothing, or accessories: their "look" tells something about them.

Specific fads come and go, but the need to establish identity comes with each new generation of adolescents.

🐦 🐦 🐦 🐦 🐦 🐦 🐦

Q *My twelve-year-old daughter reads the same books over and over. Is there something else I should be giving her?*

A Not necessarily. Preteens are going through so many changes that reading familiar books may be the only area of your daughter's life that is predictable at the moment. She might see favorite books as old, trusted friends.

If your daughter would welcome variety, I recommend *Brio* for teen girls (*Breakaway* for teen boys) from Focus on the Family (call 800-A-Family), *Campus Life* (call 800-678-6083), and *TQ* (Shepherd Ministries, 2221 Walnut Hill Lane, Irving, TX 75038-4410 or phone 214-580-8000).

🐦 🐦 🐦 🐦 🐦 🐦 🐦

Q *When I ask my boys to help around the house, they always say "I'm practicing the clarinet" or "Gotta do my homework." I don't want them to think that practicing or homework aren't important, but when the place is a mess, I think they should help.*

A Homework is important. Music practice is important, and so are chores and household responsibilities. It's not a matter of one activity being more important than another. Children need to learn the skills of time management and making choices. Being a member of a family brings privileges and responsibilities. As parents, we need to communicate this message.

Begin by writing a list of jobs and the time or date by which they must be completed. Try to vary schedules so that some jobs are done daily, weekly, or monthly. For example, if sinks need to be scoured once a week, schedule that job to be completed by Sunday evening. Or, if beds need to be made daily, you might indicate that is to be done by 8:00 A.M. on weekdays and 11:00 A.M. on weekends.

Then review with your sons exactly what is required for each chore. Allow each child to mark his first job preference; then work through the rest of the list by letting one boy choose, then the other.

If your sons feel they don't have adequate time for chores, make some suggestions. Encourage them to use flex times that are often lost in puttering, like those ten or fifteen minutes in the morning before the school bus comes. Write out possible scenarios for homework, chores, and extracurricular activities, if necessary.

🐾 🐾 🐾 🐾 🐾 🐾 🐾

Q *Do boys talk on the phone as much as girls, or is my son different? He spends most of every night on the phone.*

A Beginning in junior high, both boys and girls might spend many hours talking on the phone. Help your son balance this activity with other leisure-time options.

If you feel your son is spending too much time on the phone, ask him to keep track of his phone time for one week. Put a clock, pencil, and paper at each phone. He should write down the time he begins and ends each call. Add up the amount of time, and discuss the totals with your son. If the numbers show he really is on the phone too many hours, discuss a reasonable limit for daily phone time.

Teenagers

THIRTEEN TO EIGHTEEN YEARS OLD

* Makeup
* Stop ballet
* Computer overload
* Pay for loss?
* Disaster focus
* Expensive tastes
* Dating
* Another church's group
* Job age
* Inappropriate T-shirt
* Talking with teens
* "You don't know any-thing!"

* Curfew
* Boy/girl sleepover
* Gifts
* Party rules
* "Everybody's doing it."
* Bible on makeup
* Disappointing audition
* Earring
* Dating limits
* Conflicting behavior
* Parenting over

❦ ❦ ❦ ❦ ❦ ❦ ❦

Q My daughter is fourteen and wants to wear makeup, even though I don't. I don't want to spend money trying different brands until she finds what she likes, and don't want her to have a "free" make-over so they can sell her expensive products. Is there another alternative?

A It's good you're approaching this issue thoughtfully. For adolescents in many cultures, wearing makeup is one outward sign of growing up. During this time, your daughter needs the time and opportunity to learn about products and techniques. Here are some inexpensive ways to allow the necessary trial and error:

• Ask an adult friend to show your daughter how to apply makeup.

• Speak with your daughter's beautician. She can give general advice and suggestions without a sales pitch.

• Borrow a beauty book from the library. This will include information on skin care, which has more long-term importance than makeup has. Books are good sources, but teen magazines tend to overemphasize makeup and underemphasize the need for healthy skin routines.

• On the next sleepover, your daughter's friends can bring their makeup and attempt their own make-overs. Sharing makeup can share bacteria, so each girl should use only her own makeup.

• Your church youth group could sponsor a "females only" makeup and make-over session. This would allow your daughter and her friends to try various products without a sales pitch targeted directly at her.

• Schedule a birthday make-over for your daughter with a cosmetic company at the mall. Then, give her a cosmetics gift certificate.

🦋 🦋 🦋 🦋 🦋 🦋 🦋

Q My daughter, age fourteen, made her own decision to stop ballet after years of lessons. I told her she could continue or stop, whatever she wanted. Now she seems unhappy she quit, and I wonder if I should have decided for her.

A No, at this time in life it was really her decision. There are two parts to the decision-making process. The first part is making the actual decision. The second part is living with the choice and accepting the consequences.

This might be one of the first semi-major choices your daughter has made by herself. It's natural she would rethink the decision, whatever her choice. Give her a little time to work through her feelings, then help her reassess. Some decisions are final; others, like this one, can be changed.

🦋 🦋 🦋 🦋 🦋 🦋 🦋

Q I bought my fourteen year old a computer to use for high school homework. He loves it, but now he won't do anything else but play on the computer.

A Balance is the key. Whether the attraction is cyberspace or a video game, put a clock, pencil, and paper at the monitor. Have him record the time he begins and interrupts his computer use each day. As he logs his time, have him distinguish between time spent on assignments and time spent on recreation.

After a week, ask him to add up the figures. Evaluate the data.

Recall together how he was using that time before the computer arrived. (If he's merely skipping a few TV shows, it might be an even trade. If he has given up friends, reading, and sports, he's probably missing out on too much.)

Negotiate guidelines with your son. For example, you might decide that on school days, the computer can be used for assignments as much as necessary, plus an extra half hour for recreation. On weekends and in the summer, he can use the computer for two hours a day. Try the new schedule for a couple weeks. Then reevaluate with your son to determine if the plan brings balance to his life.

❧ ❧ ❧ ❧ ❧ ❧ ❧

Q *Is it all right to ask my fourteen year old to pay for textbooks he loses?*

A Yes. If he misplaces a book or calculator that he needs in order to keep up with his class, consider loaning him the money until he can pay it back.

❧ ❧ ❧ ❧ ❧ ❧ ❧

Q *My fourteen year old was glued to the television to watch news programs after an earthquake. Was that normal?*

A A teenager has a greater understanding about the personal and global consequences of world happenings as he moves closer to developing an adult type of thinking. Youth of exactly the same age might deal differently with the identical news story. So while your son's reaction isn't unusual, his friends didn't necessarily respond in the same way.

Encourage your teen to participate in disaster relief or community agencies that help other people. Even if aid from your area is not directed to the victims of this tragedy, teens often feel better when they can take physical action to help. Otherwise, a situation can be totally overwhelming. Positive participation channels your teen's emotions and his energy.

🐟 🐟 🐟 🐟 🐟 🐟 🐟

Q What do you do when your child has expensive tastes and you can't support them?

A There are a variety of options.

Some parents simply say, "We can't get into that." Wearing name brands is either not possible or not important. When family economics or priorities dictate, clothes labels aren't an issue.

Other parents teach children how to shop sales at local stores, designer resale shops, or name-brand outlet centers.

Other parents use this common clothing issue to help children learn personal budgeting. After teaching children to compare prices, value and quality, children are given the "base" price for a brand name the parent would ordinarily purchase. If children want the more expensive items, they are responsible for adding their own funds. This technique will work only if your child receives income from a job, birthday money, or other sources.

Here's an example:

Parent will pay for a shirt that costs twenty dollars.

Child wants a shirt that costs sixty dollars.

Options:

• Parent gives child twenty dollars, which is put into the bank until child earns the remainder. Child then buys sixty-dollar shirt.

• Parent gives child twenty dollars. Child waits until sixty-dollar shirt is clearance priced, then adds fifteen dollars and purchases the shirt at a reduced price.

💲 💲 💲 💲 💲 💲 💲

At what age should a girl start to date?

That's a judgment call for you as a parent. However, before you can even answer the question, clarify the definition of a date. For example, is a date when a boy picks up your daughter and brings her home, or is a date when she arranges in advance to meet a boy at a football game? You and your daughter might have different viewpoints, so discuss this baseline issue.

Also clarify related concerns like curfew, paying for dates, how much you need to know about where your daughter will be and what she will be doing, etc. For example, in our family, our daughters know we will ask a boy specific questions before he leaves on a date. This is simply our family procedure. We encourage our girls to alert their friends in advance.

If you personalize the dating decision to match each individual child in your family, you might consider factors like your daughter's emotional maturity, experience relating to boys in a group, means of transportation, type of event, or age of the boy.

If you set a beginning age that is consistent for all children in your family, your decision will focus on the concept of dating instead of a specific event and person.

Discuss these points before your daughter starts dating. This implies there is no specific person on which you are focusing and neither you nor your daughter will be caught up in the emotion of the moment.

✄ ✄ ✄ ✄ ✄ ✄ ✄

Q Are we wrong letting our son go with his friends to youth activities at another church?

A Your decision will be influenced by how strongly you feel about denominational and church loyalty.

Often, a teen will have more fun and be more involved if he participates with friends. If a neighboring Christian church offers a strong youth program with capable adult leaders and positive activities, it sounds like a great place for a teen to find friends and role models.

✄ ✄ ✄ ✄ ✄ ✄ ✄

Q Can my fifteen year old legally have a real paying job?

A Ask your teen to check with the guidance office at the local high school. In some states, work permits are issued for young teens if the employer and employee follow certain regulations. Often, a parent's signature is required.

✄ ✄ ✄ ✄ ✄ ✄ ✄

Q My son bought a new T-shirt with inappropriate words. He bought it with his own money, so what can I do with the shirt?

A Talk with your son. Ask why he bought the shirt. Discuss various ways the words could be interpreted and the possible meaning of the words. State your concerns.

Then discuss some ground rules for wearing the shirt. For

example, he might use it as a nightshirt or wear it around the house but not wear it in public.

❧ ❧ ❧ ❧ ❧ ❧ ❧

Q *My kids used to talk to me, but now that they are teenagers, I can't get more than a "yes" or "maybe." What am I doing wrong?*

A Perhaps nothing. Teens typically talk less with us and more with peers as their social base moves from family to friends. Try these suggestions:

• Avoid question overload. When you do ask questions, ask those that require more than a "yes" or "no," but don't pester.

• Encourage your teen to develop friendships with adults. Your teens might feel more comfortable talking to a coach or youth leader about some subjects.

• Use indirect ways to stimulate conversation. For example, talk over a hamburger after a basketball game, or comment on a radio show topic as you drive in the car. In these situations, conversation becomes a natural part of the experience, not an obvious goal.

• Plan one-on-one time. Privacy is important. Build into your schedule some alone time with your teen.

❧ ❧ ❧ ❧ ❧ ❧ ❧

Q *My daughter has been dating someone who is not good enough for her. She and I had a big fight when she said, "You don't know any-thing about love." I'm still furious about her comment. I've been married almost twenty years. How could she even think that?*

A As parents, we are often shocked by two aspects of boy/girl friendships: the intensity of teen relationships, and the pace at which teens progress to levels of serious commitment and physical entanglement. On the other hand, teens often find it impossible to imagine that we ever faced issues related to drugs, sex, or peer pressure.

Here are several suggestions:

1. Recall what it was like to be sixteen or eighteen. Do you remember the rush of feelings when a certain person looked at you or the excitement when someone passed you in the hallway? Mentally put yourself in your daughter's place to gain a greater understanding of what she feels.

2. Give opinions only when requested or when you feel it's essential to offer guidance or suggestions. This is seldom easy to do.

3. Continue communicating. When a teen is involved in a relationship we feel is inappropriate, it can dramatically impact every conversation we have with our child. Look for times you can offer an honest compliment, share a laugh, or talk about the weather.

🍎 🍎 🍎 🍎 🍎 🍎 🍎

Q *My son says he doesn't need a curfew. What do you think?*

A Even though teenagers sometimes feel "too cool" for the family circle, they still need us. We still need to determine appropriate boundaries, establish consequences for unacceptable behavior, and enforce the rules.

Discuss with your son why he feels a curfew is unnecessary. Perhaps he can monitor his own behavior in acceptable ways. If so, celebrate! Most of us hope our children will reach the time when self-discipline guides behavior.

Also discuss the benefits of a curfew with your son. You might jointly come up with a solution that's worth trying; set an appropriate time and see how that works.

As you examine this issue and others which involve setting limits, remember that rules may continue to offer a sense of security for him and for you.

❧ ❧ ❧ ❧ ❧ ❧ ❧

Q My sixteen year old wanted to go to a boy/girl sleepover after a school dance. Of course I said "Absolutely not." Have you ever heard of such a thing?

A Yes. Mixed-gender sleepovers are becoming quite common. Evidently, they started as a natural outgrowth of "safe" or "chaperoned" alternatives to unsupervised hotel-room parties for after-prom.

Teens have many opportunities for social interaction in less potentially compromising and highly charged situations. I don't see any benefit of mixed-gender sleepovers for kids of any age.

❧ ❧ ❧ ❧ ❧ ❧ ❧

Q How can I tell my aunt nicely that my son never wears the clothes she buys him for his birthday?

A Be honest when you suggest alternatives. You might explain that because your son chooses all his own clothes now, you wondered if she'd like to schedule a birthday shopping trip to the mall. This would also give her some extra time with him. If she prefers to shop on her own, suggest a store with clothing that appeals to your son.

Or, direct her to a mall that offers gift certificates redeemable at all the stores. Promise to send a photo of him wearing what he purchased with her gift money.

Explain that your son really appreciates her thoughtfulness and looks forward to her gift.

❧ ❧ ❧ ❧ ❧ ❧ ❧

Q *Is it all right to let my teenager go to a party even though I don't know the student or parents who are hosting the party?*

A Yes, if you feel the party will be safe for your teen.
When one of our teens is invited to a party, he or she knows I will phone the parent of the host. I ask two questions: Will you personally supervise the party? Will alcohol or drugs be present? I then verify the date and time. If I have never met the teen host, I usually get additional information. I find out who else has been invited, the age of the other party-goers, and if teens are bringing their own refreshments. I share the information with my teen, and we decide if the party is something he or she would like to attend.

I personally verify the factual information in this way so my teen won't think, "Mom doesn't trust me." Instead, I just want to be sure he or she is going to be in a safe environment.

❧ ❧ ❧ ❧ ❧ ❧ ❧

Q *How can I respond when my son says, "Everybody's doing it"?*

A A high school principal once told me, "I've never seen everybody do everything." She was right. I have shared her wisdom with my own teens.

"Everybody's doing it" reflects a perception. Instead of responding to your teen with another sweeping generalization, get the facts. Use your network of parents to find out how they are handling the situation. Even if other teens are "doing it," you will benefit from hearing different views.

Your personal research will tell you if "everybody is doing it." But base your decision on solid information, your own judgment, and your knowledge of your child, instead of a vague feeling.

❧ ❧ ❧ ❧ ❧ ❧ ❧

Q Does the Bible say anything about teenage girls wearing makeup?

A A variety of cosmetics are mentioned in the Bible, including ointment, perfumes, and eye paint. I could not find a specific Scripture passage which forbids or commands the use of makeup, although I Timothy 2:9 refers to modesty in public worship. Some commentaries indicate that this passage, however, cites a culturally specific example and the intent is that nothing should detract from a worshipful atmosphere.

❧ ❧ ❧ ❧ ❧ ❧ ❧

Q My daughter always had a major role in school plays. There is a new drama director this year, and my daughter only got a chorus role. She is crushed and has a hard time getting up for school every day. What can I do?

A Perhaps auditions for this play did not reflect your daughter's talent. Her lack of a leading role might have been an oversight or an attempt to give others a chance to star. Consider talking to the director just so you understand the situation.

This recent disappointment—however unwanted—offers your

daughter a chance to grow. Part of your daughter's school identity was probably defined by her involvement in theater. Now her perception of herself (and perhaps even her self-worth) and the perception of peers and faculty might be somewhat altered because of her new role as a "former" lead. A starring role was one way to be visible, but not the only way. Help her identify another area of interest at school and get immersed in that.

If she is uninterested in extracurricular options at school, suggest ways to get involved in the community. When life crashes down on teenagers, we should encourage them to look beyond themselves by looking toward others. This will be easiest for your daughter if she and a friend get involved together. Helping others will give her life meaning and help her see school as one part of the bigger picture.

Your patience, support, and encouragement are especially important during this time of growth.

My mother will be shocked if she sees her only grandson wearing an earring. Can I have him take it out before she visits?

Yes, you may certainly ask.

Am I being unfair when I tell my high school junior she can't date during the week?

That's an appropriate guideline during the school year. If your teen always respects curfew and driving rules, as the school year progresses, you might want to offer incentives for changing that dating guideline. For example: "You may go out once a week on a school night as long as your grades stay the same or go up."

❧ ❧ ❧ ❧ ❧ ❧ ❧

Q Is it odd that my teenager can lead a marching band in front of a stadium full of people but wants a good-night hug?

A Not at all. Actually, the behaviors that seem like such contrasts are totally normal. It's not unusual for a teen to effortlessly maneuver a car through traffic but be hesitant to do laundry in the basement at night because she's afraid of the dark.

These are years when our teens test the waters of independence. Teens are growing up but are not *all grown up* yet.

❧ ❧ ❧ ❧ ❧ ❧ ❧

Q Even though my teenagers live at home, I'm sad my parenting days are over. I'm not in an empty nest yet, so are my feelings normal?

A Your feelings are normal, but your parenting days aren't over. Even though you're not driving a child to T-ball games or listening to her practice a squeaky violin, you are still parenting. You have simply entered another season of parenting.

Without being aware of it, you teach every day. For example, when your teen asks, "Mom, would you ever borrow money to buy a better car?" you teach about budgeting and finance. If your teen talks about a fight after school, you might discuss problem-solving techniques.

But you do more than teach teens. You continue to shape their lives. Teenagers deal with high-stakes issues every day; they need your feedback, input, and guidance. Even if your teens physically look down on you, they emotionally look up to you.

Tomorrow, keep track of all the opportunities you have to parent. At the end of the day, reflect on your actions. I think you'll be surprised at how much parenting you do.

Section Two

GENERAL
QUESTIONS AND ANSWERS

Relationships

* New Baby
* Mourning lost dog
* Pets as friends
* Mommy's Boy
* Cutting apron strings
* Classmates teasing
* Mean talk
* Sharing
* Friend's move
* Tough question
* Explaining home situation

* Parent vs. teacher
* Social needs in home schoolers
* Family history
* Correcting another parent
* Carpool secrets
* Closely spaced children
* Last child home
* Mom or teacher?

❧ ❧ ❧ ❧ ❧ ❧ ❧

Q Our four-year-old daughter adjusted well to the birth of our son. But recently she's started to say things like, "I wish he wasn't here." What happened after things went so well?

A It sounds like your daughter has figured out her brother is really going to stay. And not only that—now that his personality is starting to show, he's a cute little guy who is starting to be heard. She can't just tuck away the baby in the corner of her mind—he's a real person. Give your daughter some time and space to work through this major change in her life.

Although it hurts to hear, "I wish he wasn't here," it's excellent that your daughter is talking about her feelings. The more she talks through her emotions, the less likely she will be to hit or act out her feelings.

You obviously did a good job to prepare your daughter for her new baby brother. You're probably doing many good things now to help her cope with reality. Here are some additional ways to remind your daughter that even though things have changed, she will always be a very special person and is loved very, very much:

• Set aside daily "alone time" for just you and your daughter, even if it's only five minutes a day. When she comes to you for help or attention at a time you're busy with the baby, suggest, "We'll read that book during our Mommy Time today. I'll look forward to it!"

• Encourage the big-girl tasks she might be moving into: choosing her own library books, buying a new backpack for preschool, selecting which clothes to wear.

• Keep her baby book handy. That will be a little visual reminder of what it was like when she was a baby.

• Do some special activities that focus on your daughter: write a story together, sing together favorite songs for a bedtime lullaby tape, take photos of you and your daughter to send to Grandma, etc.

❦ ❦ ❦ ❦ ❦ ❦ ❦

Q *Our dog ran away a couple months ago, and my daughter still misses him greatly. Is this normal?*

A Yes. Children need a good friend who will always listen, always accept them, and never make fun of them. Unfortunately, some human friends don't have these qualities. So it's not unusual when a pet becomes this "forever friend." The time line for grief varies with individual children.

❦ ❦ ❦ ❦ ❦ ❦ ❦

Q *My eleven year old is pretty much a loner but wants to get a dog. Do you think that's a good idea?*

A Yes. She won't just be choosing a pet; she'll be looking for a potential new friend.

Friendships with animals and humans can be very important, especially during these years. As parents, we need to recognize the value of those relationships and support our young adults as they develop their own patterns of socialization.

So, as you support her friendship with one of God's four-legged creatures, remember that she also might need some extra encouragement in gaining human friends. You might volunteer to drive for the next church youth-group activity. Or, offer to take your daughter and her friends out for pizza afterwards. Your support might be just the encouragement she needs to build some meaningful relationships.

❦ ❦ ❦ ❦ ❦ ❦ ❦

Q My mother-in-law accused me of raising my son as a mommy's boy. What can I do?

A Learn what you can from her, accept advice when appropriate, then go on to be the most effective mom you can. Remember that your mother-in-law is learning how to be a grandmother just as you are learning how to be a mother. She probably cares about your son and simply wants to help as much as possible.

❦ ❦ ❦ ❦ ❦ ❦ ❦

Q My dad said I should start "cutting the apron strings" with my son. I know I'm a little protective.

A Every child needs permission and space to grow up and away from us emotionally. "Cutting the apron strings" is a gradual process that continues for many years.

Healthy parent/child separation begins when we leave a child in a swimming class or day-care center. Sometimes, it's not the child but the parent who experiences separation anxiety.

If you are dealing with this issue now:

1. Recognize your feelings and then deal with them appropriately.

2. Seek opportunities for your son to grow emotionally. A child should learn to solve his own problems, cope with various personalities, and gain a sense of independence in many areas.

3. Look for ways you can grow emotionally. Attend a parenting class at your church or sign up for a child-development course hosted by a local school. By talking with other parents, you'll not only find out how they've coped with the same issue, but learn that all parents, at some time, deal with separation issues.

※ ※ ※ ※ ※ ※ ※

Q *My daughter has a learning disability and kids at school make fun of her. How can I help her make friends?*

On the playground at school, kids tease my son about being in a gifted and talented class. Is there anything I can do?

A Although these questions refer to children with different needs, both children are being socially harassed because they are "different."

First, it's great your children talked with you. You've obviously established an atmosphere in which your children feel they can talk about problems.

Children can say vicious and hateful things. However, this type of problem is less likely to appear in school environments where children are encouraged to share many kinds of gifts: an honor roll for effort, in addition to an honor roll for achievement; a craft exhibit or talent show featuring student projects; recognition for acts of kindness, in addition to trophies for those on the baseball team. When a school helps each child identify gifts and recognizes many types of talent, the whole climate becomes positive and nurturing.

Here are some general suggestions for handling the situation:

• Talk to your child's teachers. Simply say you thought they should be aware of what your child had told you. Ask for their suggestions. Also, find out if they have observed similar trouble at school. Ask for an assurance that the playground supervisor will be alerted to the problem. Let them know you'll check back in a couple weeks to see how things are going.

• Find out where and when in the curriculum your child's class deals with human relationship issues such as friendship and kindness. These topics should be part of the school curriculum at every grade level. It's terrific if your school already teaches social skills in a way that's planned, rather than incidental. If not, find out why that's not included in the curriculum.

• Arrange after-school or weekend play times for your child with individual classmates. Encourage your child to build one-on-one relationships with children. This will allow individual children to get to know your child as a person without being attached to school labels.

• Talk through a script with your child. Ask, "What can you do if this happens again?" For example, you might encourage your child to simply leave the group and start a different activity or join another group of children.

🐛 🐛 🐛 🐛 🐛 🐛 🐛

Q My daughter is a nice girl, but I overheard her talking on the phone in really mean ways about other people. What should I do?

A Sometimes children say unkind things simply because friends are talking that way. "Tearing down others to build yourself up" can be a stage.

You can take four actions:

1. Help your child feel good about herself by building on her strengths, abilities, and talents.

2. Encourage your daughter to think through situations that involve feelings. For example, you might ask, "How would you feel if the girls didn't tell you about the sleepover? How do you think Kaitlyn might feel?"

3. Encourage your daughter to move beyond cattiness by helping others. Look for opportunities for her and her friends to volunteer together in church or community activities. Positive action toward others can completely redirect group energy toward a meaningful goal.

4. Model empathy, compassion, and courtesy. When your daughter sees how you forgive someone or go out of your way to help, your behavior will speak louder than words.

🍎 🍎 🍎 🍎 🍎 🍎 🍎

Q *At what age do children begin to really share?*

A The time between one and a half and three years is when children begin to deal with sharing as a part of socialization. Sharing toys, time, and people gradually becomes part of everyday life, often between four and five years of age. Trading, taking turns, and waiting are concepts that are part of sharing.

Age, experience, basic personality of a child, the situation, and the reward all influence how and when a child shares. With sharing, practice doesn't make perfect, but once a child is two and a half, practice, positive reinforcement, and playing with peers help sharing happen.

🍎 🍎 🍎 🍎 🍎 🍎 🍎

Q *Since her best friend moved, my daughter has cried off and on. It's been several weeks. Is this normal?*

A Yes. Although the focus on adjustment and transition is often placed on the child who is leaving, not the one who is staying, both friends will cope with the loss. Try these suggestions:

1. Assure your daughter that her feelings (loss, anger, sadness) are normal. Those emotions reflect a strong friendship, which is a great blessing.

2. Listen attentively. Remember, part of having a friend is having someone to talk with. You or someone else might need to help fill that need on a temporary basis.

3. Encourage your daughter to write or phone her friend.

4. Support your daughter's development of new friends.

5. Encourage your daughter to start a journal or diary. Also, ask a librarian at the school or public library for some fiction in which characters go through a similar situation. Good books on the subject are available for children of all ages.

🐛 🐛 🐛 🐛 🐛 🐛 🐛

Q *I was driving in heavy traffic when my daughter asked, "What's the real reason you and Daddy don't live together anymore?" I've been wanting to tell her, but I stalled because it wasn't a good time to tell the whole story. Was that wrong?*

A No. Postpone a conversation when you don't know what to say, you don't have time to say what needs to be said, the place or situation isn't appropriate, or you want to consult with someone else. Children tend to ask the toughest questions when we're in the toughest situations; most parents will use stalling very effectively at some point in their lives.

Follow-up is what matters. Always combine stalling with communication that clearly says, "I *want* to talk to you about that. I *will* talk to you about that. Let's set a time to talk."

❧ ❧ ❧ ❧ ❧ ❧ ❧

Should I tell my kids' teachers that my husband and I are having marital problems?

That's your decision. A teacher wants to help your child grow and develop. Generally, the more a teacher knows about your child, the more effectively he can help.

That doesn't mean a teacher needs to know your entire family history. But if a teacher is aware of situations that affect your child and can be trusted to keep that information confidential, your child usually benefits.

❧ ❧ ❧ ❧ ❧ ❧ ❧

How can I keep a school conference from becoming a face-off between my husband and the teacher?

If you feel it would be helpful, request that the conference be scheduled at a time when a school administrator can attend. Then:

1. Prepare in advance a list of questions and concerns. During the conference, make sure your agenda concerns are addressed. Write down the ideas, suggestions, and answers so you can review them later.

2. Focus on your child. Your child is the reason you are meeting in the first place. Throughout the conversation, repeatedly seek to answer the question, "What is best for our child?"

3. Don't spend time making accusations or placing blame. Instead, work toward a solution.

4. Ask the teacher for specific ways you can help.

5. Set a time when you can get back to the teacher to assess progress.

6. Thank the teacher and administrator for their interest in your child.

❧ ❧ ❧ ❧ ❧ ❧ ❧

Q *I would like to home school when my son grows up. Should I be concerned about his social development?*

A Yes. Many home schoolers participate in area support groups which bring students together because of this reason. In some regions, home-schooling co-ops offer most of the activities found in public schools: intramural sports, bands, choirs, and clubs. School codes and rules vary, but occasionally home-school students participate in extracurricular activities at a local school and receive the rest of their instruction at home. There are obviously a variety of ways to help a home-schooled student meet social needs.

In spite of these typical activities, one veteran teacher told me that in her experience, regardless of the child, it usually takes a full year to socially integrate a home-schooled child into the classroom. A friend whose home-schooled daughters (ages nine and twelve) entered the public school says the social transition period lasted less than a week. Obviously, different experiences result in differences of opinion. The temperament of the child plays a key role in socialization and how those needs can be met.

If you choose to home school, keep in mind that your child, like all children, will need to relate to peers individually, as well as in small- and large-group settings. A child who is home schooled doesn't have different social needs than those who enroll in private or public school; however, there might be different ways in which those needs are met.

❧ ❧ ❧ ❧ ❧ ❧ ❧

Q My daughter was excited about a school assignment to do living history, but when she interviewed my uncle, she didn't get enough information for the project. She's going to try the interview again, so what should she do differently?

A Suggest your daughter take objects to trigger memories. For example, look through keepsakes to find photo albums, trinkets passed down through the years, or the family Bible, if it records important family information. Have her ask your uncle to do the same, if he has any photographs or memorabilia.

A tape recorder will help your daughter catch all the information. (Taking accurate notes on paper is difficult for even an experienced reporter.) Have her practice using the tape recorder ahead of time so that it does not become a distraction.

If your uncle seemed hesitant to talk about his personal life, suggest your daughter prepare questions about other relatives. Also, encourage her to ask concrete questions that should trigger specific answers. Here are some suggestions:

• "What's the spelling of your full name and the full names of your parents? Do you have a nickname? How did you get it?"

• "Describe your hometown. What was your favorite place there? What do you miss about it?"

• "Where did you go to school? What did you use to carry your lunch?"

• "What was the best birthday present you ever received?"

• "Who were your best friends? What was your favorite activity to do together?"

• "How did you earn money? What did you buy with the money you got?"

• "What led you to choose the type of work you do (or did)? What did you like the most? the least?"

• "How did you meet your wife?"

• "Please write down your children's names for me." (If the assignment includes a family tree, your daughter should get specific information about dates and places.)

• "What is the most wonderful place you visited? When did you go there? With whom did you go? What makes it your favorite?"

❦ ❦ ❦ ❦ ❦ ❦ ❦

Q *My younger sister and I are very close friends, but when I commented about something she did wrong as a parent, she jumped all over me. Wasn't it all right for me to tell her about the mistake so she could learn?*

A I can understand why she became defensive. I might, too, if you questioned my judgment about something that happened within my family.

However, suggestions offered with empathy are often accepted gratefully. For example, you might say, "This is what worked for me when my kids wouldn't sleep through the night . . . but I know it's tough. I remember how tired I got."

Because I'm not a perfect parent, unless the situation is potentially dangerous, I tend to keep my opinions to myself in judgment calls.

❦ ❦ ❦ ❦ ❦ ❦ ❦

Q How can I stop children in a carpool from whispering secrets? Various children get left out, and it causes hurt feelings.

A Discuss basic guidelines with the other drivers. Identify rules that you will all enforce. Explain these rules to the children when they are together in a group. Then write the rules on index cards. Clip a card to the sun visor of each car.

You might consider these guidelines:

1. Riders cannot tell secrets.

2. Riders won't discuss at whose house they're playing after school.

3. The driver of the day decides on seating arrangements.

4. Riders who break a rule are out of the carpool for a week.

Q Will my first child suffer because she is the oldest of three closely spaced children and she never had a chance to be a baby?

A Not necessarily. Birth order impacts children and their parents,* but consider these related facts:

1. Birth order is one element that helps to shape a child. Many, many other major influences also impact development.

2. Positive traits are inherent in any family position. For example, a first child might have a tendency to achieve and a strong sense of responsibility. When birth order is mentioned as a shaping influence on children, unfortunately, the focus is often on the potential negative factors.

3. We continue to develop as people and parents, just as our children grow. Perhaps you and I had similar experiences: with my first child, I had lots of energy. When our third child was born three years later, I had more mature judgment but less energy. The

strengths I brought to my parenting then helped to shape our third child.

Your birth order possibly impacted your development in both positive and negative ways. The same will be true for your children.

*Dr. Kevin Leman's classic, *The Birth Order Book* (Baker Book House Co.), is a good reference.

🐗 🐗 🐗 🐗 🐗 🐗 🐗

Q *I was looking forward to time alone with my last child before she starts school, but she's lonesome. I feel bad that I can't keep her happy.*

A If your daughter wants to be with friends, this doesn't mean you have done something wrong or that she doesn't like your company. Preschoolers are increasingly social as they near kindergarten. Talking to Mom is important, but so is playing restaurant with other four year olds.

Look at your overall plan for the next few months. You might view this year as a transitional time for both you and your daughter. Consider your personal goals, and plan ways to meet your daughter's needs.

As you look at possibilities, develop home routines you can do together: going to the store on certain days, sorting laundry, or doing routine chores at certain times. Even a simple schedule can give you both a sense of direction and purpose.

As you consider ways to meet your daughter's social, emotional, physical, and cognitive needs, look for programs with a parent component. For example, a MOPS* meeting offers learning and social activities for mothers while their preschoolers enjoy a separate program. You might find a mom-and-tot swim program at the

YMCA or a parent/child program offered by the local park district. Or, set up an informal play group.

Keep a special journal of this year. Separate this picture-and-story book into sections entitled "Time Together," "Time with Young Friends," and "Time with Others." This will be a nice keepsake for your daughter and encourage you both to enjoy many different experiences.

*You can contact MOPS, Int. (Mothers of Preschoolers, International, 1311 South Clarkson Street, Denver, CO 80210; phone 303-733-5353) for the locations of groups near you.

🍎 🍎 🍎 🍎 🍎 🍎 🍎

Q *If I home school, will I have trouble being a teacher during school hours and a mom all the other times of the day?*

A I don't know how it might affect you. However, I can share my own experience.

I taught two of my children in a public school classroom. My experiences with my son were different from those with my daughter. I don't recall significant instances when being "Mom" carried over to my son's classroom. But with my daughter, sometimes I needed to separate myself as a mom from myself as a teacher. This usually happened on days when she chose clothes that didn't match or we had an unresolved parent/child incident that was carried into the classroom. Being aware of how my feelings as a mom could influence my effectiveness as a teacher was a first step in coping with the problem. In retrospect, I was a very good teacher for my son but another teacher would have probably done a better job with my daughter.

Talk with parents who currently home school to see how they view their experience.

Chapter Seven

Behavior

- Too young to discipline?
- "No"
- Slapping
- Four-year-old dictator
- Avoiding yelling
- Sibling fights
- Bedtime-story arguments
- Telephone trouble
- Whining
- Sports crowd etiquette
- Candy rewards
- Whole group punishment
- Corporal punishment
- Intervention
- Disciplining guest
- Child at meeting
- Difficult outings
- Discussing homesickness
- Staying with grandparents
- Disobedience in public
- "Public" and "home" personalities
- Brats
- "Boys will be boys" fallacy
- Limiting playmates
- Playground fight
- Trip over toys
- Strictness
- Sarah becomes Sara

❦ ❦ ❦ ❦ ❦ ❦ ❦

Q Is a ten month old too young to discipline?

A No, not if you define the term as communicating limits in appropriate ways. A ten month old needs to learn that vertical blinds are not playthings and electric cords are not for chewing.

During these next months, your toddler will become increasingly curious. Encourage her safe explorations. When she gets near trouble spots, clearly communicate what is off-limits by using a three-step action:

1. Remove her from the area.
2. Say "no" in a stern voice.
3. Redirect her interests.

You can begin this pattern with children as young as your ten month old.

❦ ❦ ❦ ❦ ❦ ❦ ❦

Q I've gotten into a habit of saying "no" all the time to my kids. They aren't always that bad. How can I stop automatically saying "no" when they ask for something?

A It sounds like you're trying to establish a positive tone but might have fallen into a rut. That can happen so easily. You've already taken the first step to change the atmosphere: you're aware of a problem.

Just today, count the times you say "no." Every single time you say the word, make a tally mark on a piece of paper. The physical process of using paper and pencil will help you monitor your own behavior.

At the end of today, recall specific situations in which you used the word *no*. Look for patterns. Then, for starters, isolate one type of situational pattern and work to change it. Here's an example:

Your child tosses sand and you automatically say, "No, you can't throw sand." Mentally plan a different way to communicate the same message. For example, next time you might say, "Keep the sand in the sandbox."

Remember that there still will be times when "no" is an appropriate response. Don't be afraid to use that word; just use it more selectively.

Q My toddler thinks we're playing patty-cake when I slap her hands after she does something wrong. If I slap harder, she cries and I feel bad.

A Instead of the slap, substitute some of these actions:
 • Redirect behavior away from trouble. That will be easiest if you rotate toys and books regularly. Your daughter will always have "new" and interesting playthings.

 • Set up a consistent pattern. If you don't want your daughter to throw things down the toilet, follow the same pattern of words and actions every time you observe this behavior.

 • Use "no." Say the word firmly and with meaning. But use "no" only when necessary. Save the word for when you want to communicate "Absolutely not. Never!" When "no" becomes an automatic response, the importance of its meaning is diminished.

 • Use humor. Lighten the moment with a smile, a joke, or a laugh. You might say, "You silly little thing! We'll give you a bath tonight; not now."

• Develop your own list of techniques that work. Post it on the refrigerator as a reminder of alternatives for coping with problem situations.

Q What do you do with a four year old who runs the house and everyone in it?

A It's good you want to change this pattern of behavior now. Begin to restore a sense of order by setting limits. Make rules that are appropriate for the child and your household. Enforce the limits firmly and consistently. Isolate one behavior at a time. Then reward positive behavior, and move on to another out-of-bounds action.

I would also suggest you enroll in a parenting course. That will help you identify why and how a four year old started running the household in the first place! Phone the office of your pediatrician, your church, or a local school or day-care center for class suggestions. Also, check the parenting section of your church or public library for some helpful resources.

If necessary, seek professional advice. For us to grow as parents, we often must step back and review our own actions and attitudes. Sometimes this is easier to do with additional help.

Q How can I avoid yelling at my kids?

A I'm not sure any of us can totally avoid it, but when you really want a child to listen, whisper. That technique is often used by classroom teachers, but it works just as well in the kitchen.

Also, make sure the tone of your child management is positive. Catch your children being good. This technique is effective for children of all ages. When you expect and affirm good behavior, you'll find that both you and your children will smile more and yell less.

Yelling implies a possible difference of opinion. It's appropriate that much in a child's world is controlled by adults, but children should be encouraged to make decisions whenever appropriate. For example, they can choose, perhaps within limits, what to wear (the red or blue shorts) and when to make their beds (anytime before 11:00 A.M.). A child who makes some decisions is often more receptive to following adult directions at other times.

Also make eye contact with your children whenever possible. This will avoid those times of inevitable yelling across the house when you call, "Did you walk the dog?" and five minutes later you call again, "Did you walk the dog?" Fifteen minutes later your child will complain he never heard you. Eye contact can prevent a lot of yelling.

Q How can I prevent my boys from fighting with each other?

A Signs of sibling rivalry are a fact of life if you have more than one child. That rivalry increases for same-sex children and for closely spaced children.

Young children tend to act out instead of talk through their problems. As children grow up, they should learn verbal problem-solving. For example, when your son is punched by his brother, you can encourage him to respond, "I'm angry you stepped on my toe. That hurt." Modeling an actual script like this can defuse problems.

But I also suggest you do something that's tough: Avoid getting involved. Very often as parents, we tend to side with the younger child or the child whom we perceive is weaker. This prevents our children from learning how to work through their own problems. Unless a child is being physically harmed, it's usually best to walk away from the situation, saying, "You boys know how to talk through your differences. You solve the problem."

In everyday parenting, we sometimes encourage sibling rivalry. For example, it's easy to set up a situation that can trigger problems. Avoid saying, "Jordan cleaned up his room so nicely. Why don't you?" Instead, give Jordan a specific compliment. Later, in a different setting, ask your other son about cleaning his room.

One of the best ways to prevent unnecessary sibling rivalry is to encourage each child to develop his own areas of interest and competence. It's all right if only one boy wants to play baseball. Encourage each one to make individual choices. Do everything possible so that both boys have areas in which they can shine.

❧ ❧ ❧ ❧ ❧ ❧ ❧

Q *I want to read my children a bedtime story, but they can never agree on a book. After I finally read one book, they want more, and I'm too tired to argue. They go to bed upset regardless of how much I read, and I'm mad because they get to bed so late.*

A Add some structure to the reading time by solving the three most common problems:

• If children have trouble selecting a book, offer them specific options.

• If one child's choice consistently "wins" and is read, have the children take turns. Simply track choices on a piece of paper stuck on the refrigerator.

• If children want "just one more book," set a limit on the maximum reading time before the first page is turned.

🦋 🦋 🦋 🦋 🦋 🦋 🦋

Q *My children are fairly well-behaved, until I answer the telephone. Then they are terrible!*

A Establish a basic rule: Children are not to bother a parent when he is talking on the telephone, except in an emergency.

Discuss in advance the options for your child while you are on the phone. Keep some special toys in a specific place—within reach of your long phone cord—just for use while you're on the phone. You might even label these "*telephone toys*," as I did when my children were very young.

Select quiet items that don't require adult supervision or another child. You might include special pop-up or sticker books, cassette tape and book sets, colored pencils, and various kinds of creative drawing materials.

Then as you go to answer the next phone call, remind your child of the new pattern by saying something like, "Great. Now you get to select a phone toy." This first time, keep the conversation short. Finish the call at a later time, if necessary. Help your child put away the telephone toy when you hang up.

Positively reinforce your child, especially after the first few times you use this new plan. Reading a book together is one of the best ways to tell a child, "You did a good job."

Help your child succeed. Look at the amount of time you spend on the phone. You may need to talk less or find better times to make calls. For example, don't begin a long phone call when your child is hungry. That just spells disaster.

🐌 🐌 🐌 🐌 🐌 🐌 🐌

Q *My daughter is so whiny, I can hardly stand to be around her.*

A When your daughter starts whining, simply say, "Talk normally, and I'll be glad to listen."

Some children and preadolescents get into a habit of using a particular tone of voice and aren't even aware of it. Your comment will alert your daughter to the problem and the need to change.

🐌 🐌 🐌 🐌 🐌 🐌 🐌

Q *The last two weekends, I've been embarrassed at how other parents yell at the referees and scream at the basketball coach. Is there anything that can be done?*

A As the mother of two teenage soccer referees, I appreciate your comment. Parents on the sidelines can probably receive an infraction card of some sort if the referee observes a blatant problem. However, I'd seek out the school or league administrator and see if preventative action can be taken before the next game.

Everyone on the sidelines should follow what I call the basic rules for parents at all children's events: Be there, be respectful, be supportive.

🐌 🐌 🐌 🐌 🐌 🐌 🐌

Q *What do you think of giving kids candy as a reward for "good" behavior, like sleeping through the night or getting good grades?*

A When trying to change a child's action pattern using a "behavior modification technique," many parents use tangible rewards. For example, during toilet training, a parent might give a child a sticker every time he uses the potty. As the behavior changes, improves, or decreases, tangible rewards are replaced by verbal affirmation, such as saying, "That's great."

We should support our child's move toward self-reliant, socially acceptable behavior. Sometimes behavior modification and a system of rewards are helpful; sometimes, it's an unnecessary crutch. We must decide based on the child and the situation.

🍎 🍎 🍎 🍎 🍎 🍎 🍎

Q *What can I do when my daughter's teacher insists on punishing her whole class when only a few kids act up?*

A It is seldom appropriate to punish everyone because of actions by a few. The reason goes back to the goals of child management: to help a child learn to distinguish between right and wrong, to support a child's move toward self-discipline, and to affirm a child who follows the rules. A child should be affirmed for appropriate behavior, not punished.

Occasionally, it's impossible to identify an individual student who has caused trouble. This can happen when a teacher walks into a generally disruptive classroom or if there's a fight on the school bus and no one will talk about what happened.

Talk with your child's teacher or school administrator. Approach it from the perspective, "This is what I hear from my child. How can I help my child who feels she's been treated unfairly?"

🐁 🐁 🐁 🐁 🐁 🐁 🐁

Q *I heard a mother tell a fussy child in the grocery store, "Do you want me to go get the fly swatter?" I was shocked that she'd threaten a child like that. What do you think?*

A I think it's relatively easy to criticize another parent. Before you or I had children, we probably said, at one time or another, "When I'm a parent, I'll never do that." Yet we've quite possibly done something very similar. The threat of corporal punishment was not the best way to handle the situation.

🐁 🐁 🐁 🐁 🐁 🐁 🐁

Q *During a meeting at school, a parent smacked her child several times. Should any of us have done or said anything?*

A A parent is responsible for monitoring a child's behavior. It would be inappropriate for another person to admonish the parent. However, if the child was obviously disruptive and the parent did not leave with the child, you could have whispered to the parent your personal offer to care for the child out of the room.

🐁 🐁 🐁 🐁 🐁 🐁 🐁

Q *Should I discipline children who are disobedient at our house, even when their mother is standing there and just watches them?*

A Each family sets its own limits of acceptable behavior. Some families might have broader boundaries than you're accustomed to, but it's awkward when guests don't monitor the behavior of their own children.

If necessary, simply state the rules. For example, you might say, "At our house, the sand stays in the box and feet stay out. That's the way we do it here." That shows the adult and child guests that you expect them to follow the same rules your own children obey.

Remember that real out-of-bounds behavior often occurs when a child wants attention. Some days it's not realistic to have an adult conversation when children are running around. You might simply say, "Let's continue talking tonight. I'll phone you after the kids are in bed. Play is just getting too wild right now, and I think my children need to go inside."

S S S S S S S

Q *The only way I can attend a meeting for church volunteers is to take my four year old with me, but last time I did that, lots of people gave me dirty looks. What should I do?*

A You must decide if the place and event will be appropriate for a child. It's always questionable whether or not to take a child to an adults-only meeting.

Sometimes the format is informal, and children can attend if they read or play quietly at the back of the meeting room. Often, it's just not appropriate for a child to be included.

Contact the meeting organizer. Present your dilemma.

Most groups that ask for parent volunteers either provide childcare or conduct business in a way that does not require meeting attendance.

❦ ❦ ❦ ❦ ❦ ❦ ❦

Q *My kids act bad when I try to take them somewhere special. How can I avoid this kind of trouble?*

A Try these ideas:

1. Plan an outing when children are rested and fed, and during times when they would normally be awake. Some parents schedule errands during nap time, so children will fall asleep, but this backfires when children stay awake during the errands and then are crabby because they haven't had enough sleep.

2. Be realistic. Sibling rivalry and jealousy come along with children wherever they go. Just because you climb into a car doesn't mean your children will be on their best behavior.

3. Inform your children of plans in advance, even if you give only general guidelines. For example, "We're going to buy Katherine a new pair of shoes and then go to the grocery store." Children generally behave better when they know what is planned.

4. Discuss your expectations. State very clearly that you anticipate the children will behave appropriately, and specify exactly what that means. For example, "Katherine, you may choose a new pair of shoes. Cory, when we go to the grocery store, you may push the cart. Do you have any questions?"

5. Ask your children for input. "Going someplace special" might mean something totally different to you than to your children. When appropriate, encourage their participation in setting agendas and making plans.

❦ ❦ ❦ ❦ ❦ ❦ ❦

Q *If I bring up the subject of being homesick when my son spends two weeks away from home, will that encourage him to get homesick?*

A No, not if the issue is simply one of many pre-trip things you discuss. Don't focus on homesickness; simply discuss the topic in a matter-of-fact tone of voice during normal trip preparations.

When parents raise potentially sensitive issues like this, children often appreciate that the situation has been brought out into the open. You might simply say, "Sometimes children miss home when they're away. Talk to your dad about how you feel. If you do get a little homesick, that's normal. Sometimes I get homesick when I'm on business trips. I work through my feelings by using exercise equipment at the hotel."

Using this kind of script says to your child: "It's all right if you feel this way. I feel this way, too, sometimes. You can handle the situation."

❦ ❦ ❦ ❦ ❦ ❦ ❦

Q *Do you have any suggestions that will help my children act better when we stay overnight at my in-laws'? Although the children take along toys, they seem to get bored and into trouble very quickly.*

A Part of the stress for children staying in another house is that they don't have things to "mess around with." The other problem is that, typically, children have little to do while adults talk. Minimize both these problems with advance planning.

Here are some possibilities:

• Bring along their bicycles or skates so they can blow off steam where it's least likely to be disruptive—outside.

• Give them paint brushes and buckets of water to "resurface the driveway." Plain water turns blacktop or concrete into a totally different color (until the next rain).

• Ask Grandma to start saving items with the potential to become great creatures and creations: cardboard rolls, empty boxes of all sizes, string, yarn, bits of wrapping paper, old greeting cards, magazines, catalogs, etc. Bring along children's scissors and glue sticks. When you arrive, cover the kitchen table with newspaper or a paper tablecloth, and encourage the children to create. At the end of the visit, projects can be thrown away or saved as masterpieces.

• Give the children a specific project to complete during the visit. For example, you might ask them to tape record favorite songs on a cassette, or tell a scary story. Then you can all listen to their tape. Date the tape, and save it to listen to on a later visit. This might start a tradition and become a piece of living history for your family.

Also, roll small gifts into their sleeping bags. A promised surprise can encourage appropriate behavior.

Q The mother waiting in front of me at the store simply said, repeatedly, "Joshua, don't do that" during Joshua's almost continual disobedience while she was checking out. Shouldn't she have done something to stop him?

A In a public place, a parent should stop inappropriate behavior while attracting as little attention as possible. This is often easier to say than to do.

After the mom clearly communicated "no," she might have followed up with a distraction technique. For example, she might have said, "Stand down here, and count how many different items come off the conveyor belt." To follow up with a physical activity, she might have said, "Joshua, you can collect the dog food and put it in this brown bag." To change the emotional tone, she might have said, "Would you like macaroni and cheese for lunch or vegetable soup?"

Sometimes, it is necessary to physically remove a child.

After a public incident like this, a parent needs to clarify the difference between acceptable and unacceptable behavior, explaining the consequences of inappropriate behavior in the future. Then, before the next shopping trip, the parent and child should review expectations and appropriate behavior.

❧ ❧ ❧ ❧ ❧ ❧ ❧

Q *Why would the teachers say my daughter is quiet at school when I know how noisy she is at home?*

A She probably is quiet at school!

Some children put so much pressure on themselves to show a "school behavior," they tend to let down after school with wild, noisy, or almost out-of-bounds behavior. In such instances, the pressure often comes from within the child and is not the result of something parents said or did to make the child act that way.

Sometimes, in our desire to encourage good school behavior, we unconsciously program our children to be quiet. Have you ever told your child, "Now listen to the teacher" or "Behave yourself today"? Those well-meaning statements might signal to a child, "At school you must be quiet."

So some children quite naturally perceive that good school behavior is being quiet.

Some children are afraid to speak or contribute answers because they fear being wrong or being made fun of. A healthy classroom atmosphere will encourage appropriate participation by all children. But some children will always be quieter in school than at home—and most teachers appreciate that!

❧ ❧ ❧ ❧ ❧ ❧ ❧

Q *My husband and I have friends whose children are brats. I'm afraid their kids are going to ruin our nice adult relationship.*

A Schedule family projects that might benefit each family. Hosting a seasonal cleanup of each family yard or hosting a joint garage sale will model cooperation. There will be numerous opportunities to positively reinforce the behavior and efforts of all children.

Also, plan activities that offer open-ended play possibilities for the children. Or go sightseeing where your families could be together but have lots of individual freedom. Check your local newspaper for suggestions of "day trips." Look for a historic site, farm, or outdoor museum.

Some families reserve rooms for the same weekend at a motel. Select a place with many indoor activity options for the children: an indoor pool, games, or miniature golf. You can share family devotions, Bible-story reading, and prayers.

Also, consider some "adult only" events. If you and your husband enjoy these people, children don't always need to be involved.

※ ※ ※ ※ ※ ※ ※

Q *When another mother saw me watching her misbehaving child, she caught my eye and said, "Boys will be boys." I couldn't believe she excused bad behavior just because her child was a male.*

A The comment, "Boys will be boys" is completely irrelevant. Boys and girls of all ages need consistent, appropriate limits along with adult guidance, affirmation, and models of socially acceptable behavior.

※ ※ ※ ※ ※ ※ ※

Q *How can I stop a badly-behaved neighbor child from playing with my daughter?*

A Be kind, but direct, as you talk individually with your child, the neighbor child, and the parent of the neighbor child. You might simply say, "Play doesn't seem to be going well right now, so I'm going to take a breather before the children play together again."

If this is truly a bad situation, you need to prevent contact, at least temporarily.

※ ※ ※ ※ ※ ※ ※

Q *My boy got into a fight at school, and I don't know who to believe: the playground supervisor, his friends, or him.*

A You might never find out what really happened, because even if each person reports the truth, it will reflect what each saw from his own perspective. If your son is aware of how the problem could have been handled differently, then that's what counts.

❧ ❧ ❧ ❧ ❧ ❧ ❧

Q *My son throws a fit when I ask him to pick up big castles and huge garages that he makes with toys, but I simply can't allow him to leave them in the middle of the living room. What can I do?*

A Occasionally, set aside space where long-term projects can be left undisturbed. A child's creativity can be stimulated when he has the opportunity to think about his play over a longer period of time and he can develop much more elaborate play themes and ideas.

Even when you offer this expanded play opportunity, it's appropriate to set reasonable limits. You might say, "I see you're getting out all those pillows and blankets again. If you want to build another fort, you may keep it up overnight in that corner, but everything must be put back before lunch tomorrow."

❧ ❧ ❧ ❧ ❧ ❧ ❧

Q *I'm not as strict with my children as my parents were with me. Is my child having too easy a life?*

A Being strict is not the critical element in child management. Consistency and using appropriate techniques are far more important.

There are trade-offs with each generation. Children today have an easier life in some respects than we did. But they might face tough decisions regarding sex, drugs, and alcohol at an age when we were still buying baseball cards.

Parents today still try to nurture children to grow up with Jesus and become contributing members of society. That goal doesn't change with strictness of discipline or the calendar year.

🐞 🐞 🐞 🐞 🐞 🐞 🐞

Q *My daughter Sarah wants to change the spelling of her name to Sara. How do I react?*

A Your question, "How do I react?" might be exactly why your daughter raised the issue in the first place. Sometimes our children test us even though they aren't consciously aware that they're doing it. Your daughter might be trying to see how you'll react. Or, she might consider a different spelling as a way of establishing individual identity. That's one of the reasons some children like nicknames.

The next time she raises the issue, you might explain why you chose her name with that particular spelling. I wouldn't invest a lot of emotional energy on this issue. If she chooses to spell her name differently or use a nickname, that's her choice.

I would not even mention changing her name on school records. If she still feels strongly about the subject ten or fifteen years from now, she can take legal action to make that change official.

Chapter Eight

Wellness

- Allergies
- Smoke-filled preschool
- Suspected abuse
- Toy recalls
- Convalescence
- Return-to-school overload
- Honesty on health form
- TV nightmares
- First sex questions
- Simple sex talk
- Uneasy discussing sex
- Repeat sex talk
- Cautious or fearful?
- Boys in restroom
- Car seats
- Car door accidents
- Bike helmets
- Appealing breakfasts
- Trading school lunches
- Candy awards
- Safe pool?
- Play set safety
- Playground injury
- Unsafe park
- Neighborhood safety
- Permissiveness
- Back-to-school tiredness
- Healthy tan?
- Lifeguard precautions
- Sunburn
- Wearing glasses

❧ ❧ ❧ ❧ ❧ ❧ ❧

Q *My daughter has allergies. She came home in tears from a birthday party because she couldn't eat the food. What do you suggest?*

A Allergies aren't fun. When a child wears glasses, is diagnosed with auditory attention deficit, or faces any beyond-the-ordinary challenge, she learns at an early age that life isn't fair.

Here are some ways to help her cope:

1. Listen. Encourage her to talk about how she feels.

2. Plan ahead. Before the next party, phone the party host to learn the menu. Offer to bring alternate foods for your daughter. This can prevent her from incorrectly generalizing, "I can't eat anything."

3. Support. It's great your daughter self-monitors her food choices. Both you and your daughter's doctor can keep her informed on expanding possible food options.

4. Keep the problem in perspective. Emphasize what your daughter *can* eat instead of what she *can't* eat. This will help her understand that allergies are a hassle and an inconvenience, but she can live with them.

❧ ❧ ❧ ❧ ❧ ❧ ❧

Q *Sometimes when I pick up my son from day care, he smells like a smokestack. Are day-care people allowed to smoke around children?*

A That's a good question, especially because there's growing concern about the dangers to children of second-hand smoke. Usually, smoking is not allowed in food-preparation areas or in child-care areas when children are present.

Phone your local child-care licensing agency to find out how the standards read in your area. Then discuss the issue with the child-care director.

❧ ❧ ❧ ❧ ❧ ❧ ❧

Q   *What should I do if I think a child is being abused?*

A   Your local police department can refer you to a designated hotline in your area.

Calls can be made anonymously and records are usually confidential.

It's helpful to give specific details about a risky or potentially dangerous situation. For example, you might share information about a fourth-floor window without a screen, sounds of violence against a child, or a child being left alone for a long period of time. Don't personally investigate a situation.

❧ ❧ ❧ ❧ ❧ ❧ ❧

Q   *There are so many toy recalls. How can I buy only safe toys?*

A   I hear the frustration in your question. It's discouraging to see a favorite toy from a popular company appear on a recall list. Although we can't know all the hazards—stuffing with a potentially harmful fiber, for example—we must be alert to obvious problems. For example, babies shouldn't be given any toy with buttons. Buttons of all kinds, even those painted to look like eyes for a cuddly teddy bear, can be easily removed and become a choking hazard.

Age guidelines printed on packages are just that: guidelines. Establish your own safety standards, then share them with grandparents or others who purchase gifts for your child. Your personal standards will probably be far more stringent than those regulated.

Be especially cautious with garage sale purchases and hand-me-downs: original tags and warning labels may have faded or been removed.

❧ ❧ ❧ ❧ ❧ ❧ ❧

Q *Once a sick child starts to feel better, I feel worse because he's so hard to care for. Help!*

A Use these tips to make a child's recovery easier:
• Change the place. If a bedroom is the major sickroom site, change rooms. A recuperating child can draw at a dining room table or sit in the living room. This also gives you a chance to change the sheets or air out his bedroom.

• Prop up a child to look outside. Four walls get so confining. Encourage activities that will mentally take him beyond the room. For example, set up your child to look out the window, and put a cassette with a blank tape next to the chair. Your child can tape a list of things he sees that move with wheels or fly with wings, or he can catalog things of various colors or one object beginning with each letter of the alphabet. Perhaps your child can record a story about "The day our maple tree started talking" or "When the sidewalk walked away." He can share the tape with other family members at the end of the day.

• Take breaks when possible. If someone can watch your child for a few minutes, get out, even if it's just for a walk around the block. Accept help from anyone who offers. This is not the time to play superparent.

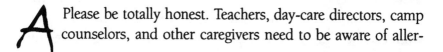

Q *Why do teachers pile on homework the first day a child returns to school after being sick? I think the burden is too much for my son.*

A The main reason a teacher would want a student to "hurry and catch up with us" is that the work done today was probably based on concepts presented when the child was absent. Or, perhaps a test is scheduled, and the teacher wants to be sure your son has the necessary material.

There are two ways you and your child can prevent this situation from happening again.

When you report your child's absence to the school office, ask the secretary to leave a note in his teacher's mailbox, requesting that homework assignments be left in the office. You can pick up the work later in the day or arrange for your child's assignments to be sent home with a student who lives nearby.

Another approach puts the responsibility on your child even before he gets sick. Ask your child to get the name and phone number of a dependable student in each class. Then he can contact these people directly and keep up with class work as his health improves.

Q *How honest should I be on my child's school health form? I don't want teachers to label him as weird because of his small medical problem.*

A Please be totally honest. Teachers, day-care directors, camp counselors, and other caregivers need to be aware of allergies, frequent ear infections, or other problems, as well as medications.

I taught in an elementary school where a child had a seizure on the playground. When school personnel tried to help the child by looking on his medical form for medication or treatment information, there were only blank spaces. We later learned the child had suffered from seizures for years and was on medication, but his mother never included that important information because she didn't want people to think he was "different."

Q *My daughter has had nightmares ever since she watched a graphic report on "safety in the streets." Am I wrong to keep her away from television for a while?*

A Not necessarily. You know your daughter. If she tends to internalize news stories, it might be better to temporarily shield her from the vivid nature of television reports. During this time, she might see a real news story and create a totally different scenario in her imagination. Continue to talk with her, though. Answer her questions. Reassure her as needed. And if the nightmares continue, seek professional help.

Q *At what age do you start talking to a child about sex?*

A As parents, we actually begin teaching about sex when they are very young. After all, our children see us interact with members of the opposite sex, they see how we react when we receive a wedding announcement or hear of a friend getting divorced, and they see our adult bodies when we change into a swimsuit in the locker room at the pool.

Specific conversations about sex usually begin when we respond to a preschool-level question, "How did I get born?" The benefit of following your children's lead in answering their questions is that you will always hit the subject at their level of interest. At what point children actually ask you about sex will depend on their peer group, media influences, experiences, curiosity level, and relationship with you.

However, if your children don't ask questions about sex, you should raise the issue. As individual parents, we determine the best time, although many parents share the basic facts of life around the age of eight or nine.

Q Is there an easy way to talk about sex to a child?

A Just apply the basics of good communication:
 • Be honest, even if it means saying, "I don't know."
 • Use correct terminology.
 • Encourage your child to ask questions.
 • Maintain eye contact.
The first time you talk about sex, both you and your child will feel more relaxed if you have a private place in which to talk.

Q I'm uncomfortable talking about sex, but I know I should give my kids the basics.

A Yes, we should talk with our children about sex. After all, we aren't just stating facts. We are sharing information within a set of values. Your attitude toward sex will be as important as the information.

There are several ways to increase your comfort level with the topic:

1. Relearn the basic facts. Then write down the information you want to tell your child. Practice your speech out loud or in front of a mirror, if you wish. This will build your confidence.

2. Find out what your child has learned at school. Get a copy of the health-education curriculum. Then you can begin by restating what your child should have already learned. Simply reviewing facts, instead of presenting new concepts, will build a shared base of information for the two of you.

3. Consider various formats. You might watch a video together, or you might ask your child to read a pamphlet that you can discuss later. This approach allows you to share the information but tends to reduce the pressure.

If you are still uncomfortable, be honest about that. You might say, "I'm a little nervous talking to you about sex, but it's such an important subject, I really want to discuss it with you." Most children will respond well to such an honest approach.

🕊 🕊 🕊 🕊 🕊 🕊 🕊

Q My son is asking the same questions about sex I've answered before. Is he doing this just to torment me?

A Perhaps, but probably not. With questions about God, sex, money, relationships, and other sensitive topics, once is not enough. You'll face identical or similar issues as your child grows up.

Sometimes children think about an answer over a long period of time. Often, they simply want to confirm what they think you said, because they recently heard different information (or misinformation). Or, your child might want to ask a basic question with the hope that you'll provide more in-depth answers now that he's older.

Think of the bright side: your personal comfort level in talking about these issues will increase as your child grows up. And best of all, he's still coming to you with his questions. That's a real tribute to your relationship.

❧ ❧ ❧ ❧ ❧ ❧ ❧

Q How can I teach my twelve year old to be cautious but not have her become overly frightened?

A Discuss strategies for handling certain situations. Talk through some "what if?" scenarios. Always preface these discussions by saying, "This will probably never happen, but if it does, let's talk about ways you can handle it."

For example:

• "What if something happens at the party that makes you uncomfortable?" (Should she phone you? Should she wait and see if anything else happens? Should she pair up with a friend she trusts?)

• "What if someone who's picking up a friend from school offers to drive you home?" (Should she phone you for permission from the school office? Can she ride with certain parents? What about caregivers or older siblings?)

• "What if she is waiting for the bus before school and a driver stops his car next to her and asks for money?" (Should she run back inside your house and risk missing the bus? Should she say

"No" and back away?)

Talking through real-life scenarios will give your child a chance to think about her responses, show her that you care about keeping her safe, and help her become safety conscious. This kind of practice will also help her realize there are often several possible solutions in a situation.

🍂 🍂 🍂 🍂 🍂 🍂 🍂

Q *My sons are three and five, but am I wrong to still take them with me to the women's rest room when I'm shopping?*

A It's fine to take them with you. We're responsible for our children's safety.

As your sons get older, another option might be to ask your older son to open the door to the men's rest room and check if anyone is inside. If the room is empty, the boys can enter together while you wait right at the outside door.

🍂 🍂 🍂 🍂 🍂 🍂 🍂

Q *How can I keep my two year old in her car seat?*

A First, eliminate potential problems with the seat. Cover a vinyl seat with a cloth. Even when temperatures are cool, vinyl can stick to bare legs. In warm weather, take along a towel to protect the entire seat or belt parts from the hot sun. Also, check that nothing is poking out of the car seat.

Be sure the seat belt and car seat are properly sized for your child. It's easy to see when shoes or diapers don't fit, but we don't always think about children outgrowing a car seat or belt adjustment.

Before you load the car next time, firmly state to all riders that the car will move when everyone's seat belt is fastened. If your child wiggles out of the belt, pull over to the side of the road and stop the car. Be firm and consistent: the car moves only when seat belts are in place.

There are some items that might help keep your child buckled. For years, we had a "seat belt buddy" attached with Velcro on one seat belt. Or, your child can strap in a doll or stuffed toy before you strap in the child. A play bag, hooked over the front seat within easy reach of the child might also help. But these are just extras. It's your enforcement of the seat belt rule that really counts.

✄ ✄ ✄ ✄ ✄ ✄ ✄

Q *After one smashed fingernail and another near miss, how can we prevent children's fingers from getting caught in car doors?*

A Some families allow only adults to close and open car doors. You might develop a routine in which the adult says, "Hands on laps." Only then, after carefully checking that all hands are in laps, does the adult close the door. Other families permit only one designated child to close doors.

Be especially careful on windy days, when doors slam shut by themselves.

✄ ✄ ✄ ✄ ✄ ✄ ✄

Q *My daughter wants to ride her bike to school but doesn't want kids to see her helmet. I don't want kids to make fun of her, but I've always insisted she wear a helmet when she rides.*

A This shouldn't be a problem because your school should support you. Every school should not only provide a safe place to store helmets, but require that all bikers use a bike lock and wear a helmet. Unfortunately, these are not standard procedures everywhere.

Please show this page to your administrator: I'm sure he'll be pleased you care about safe biking and will take steps to amend school procedures.

In addition, your parent group can sponsor a bike clinic, or even sell bike helmets as a fund-raiser. Some parent groups sponsor family events like an annual all-school bike hike, when students see their teachers and other role models wearing helmets.

These additional activities support a climate of safe biking, which always includes wearing a helmet.

🐝 🐝 🐝 🐝 🐝 🐝 🐝

Q How can I get breakfast into my son before he leaves for school?

A Research consistently shows the importance of a nutritious breakfast, so it's important to deal with the issue of hesitant morning eaters.

Your son might not be a morning eater; if so, you probably noticed the fact even when he was an infant. His first good feeding might have been long after the usual "baby breakfast hour."

It's also possible your son just doesn't like typical breakfast foods. Instead of cereal and orange juice, serve leftover pizza or another healthful food choice.

Drinking good nutrition might be more appetizing than chewing at 7:00 A.M. Mix up a vitamin-loaded shake.

Is your son slow to get going in the morning? Perhaps setting the alarm slightly earlier would give him a little extra time before eating.

Also, check the morning schedule to be sure there aren't other problems. Children can offer various reasons to skip breakfast. For example: "If I don't eat, I don't have to brush my teeth" or "If I don't eat, I get to watch more TV." Some children stop to munch breakfast from a local quick store on the walk to school. Consider these possibilities.

Then share your concern with your son. Come up with a joint solution.

🍎 🍎 🍎 🍎 🍎 🍎 🍎

Q *How can I stop my son from trading away part of his school lunch?*

A It can be a shock the first time we hear that our children regularly trade their piece of fresh fruit for a bag of greasy chips, but it's a sad fact of school life.

If your son is able to pack, or partially pack, his own lunch, he's likely to eat it. Visit school during the lunch hour someday. Look at how much food children actually eat, various ways of packing foods, the length of time for eating, and the tone of the cafeteria. This can give you a realistic view of lunch at school. If you observe problems, volunteer to serve on or start a school nutrition committee.

Then ask your son to write or dictate a list of what he'd like to eat. Simply fold a paper in quarters. He can write specific foods into each category: drink, main course, fruit/veggie, dessert or snack treat.

Children who eat at school typically gobble their food, then race to the playground. As parents, we tend to put much more time, more food, and more emotional energy into lunches than is necessary. It's a situation worth discussing, but it's not worth a great deal of concern. Serving nutritious meals at home helps to balance less-than-adequate lunches at school.

❧ ❧ ❧ ❧ ❧ ❧ ❧

Q How can I get my son's teacher to give awards that aren't candy? My problem is a 120-pound fifth grader who is overweight and is seriously trying to do something about it.

A It's reasonable to anticipate that any reward system will propel students toward excellence and affirm them in healthy, wholesome ways. It's also easy to fall into the habit of using food as a reward.

In the classroom, earning bonus points is probably the most common noncandy award at any grade level. A student might work toward a goal, perhaps toward a "free" night without homework or bonus points on a test. Sticker charts or the opportunity to choose from a "treasure chest" are effective motivational aids in the primary grades.

As children move to the middle grades, time with a teacher can be more coveted than any candy bar. Junior high teachers are typically very talented at getting awards in the form of gift certificates and product coupons for nonfood items from local businesses.

Share your concern, and perhaps some of these suggestions, with your son's teacher.

❧ ❧ ❧ ❧ ❧ ❧ ❧

Q How can I know if the city pool is safe for my children? I can't very well walk up to the lifeguard and ask, "Is your pool safe for my kids? I've got a little one who swallows water."

A Each state has its own regulations for public pools. Contact your local office of public health for information on pools in your area.

★ ★ ★ ★ ★ ★ ★

Q *How deep should bark be underneath a play set?*

A The preferred amount of energy-absorbent material is twelve to sixteen inches, although a depth of at least eight inches will help to cushion a fall.

★ ★ ★ ★ ★ ★ ★

Q *When my son was injured at recess, I was called to the school. As I walked him across the playground to the car, I was shocked at the wild behavior of the students. How can I protect him from that zoo of children?*

A Every child is entitled to a safe school environment, so begin by talking to the principal about adult supervision. Ask, "Is more help needed? Can the adults in charge see all areas of the playground?"

If additional help is needed, the principal can work with the parent organization or a local senior citizens' group to provide more supervision. The school administrator can schedule training sessions in child development, playground games, first aid, and emergency procedures for the volunteers.

If the children do not have enough play equipment to keep busy and happy, talk to the playground supervisor, teachers, or parent group. Perhaps a certain amount of money can be collected (through cake walks, plant sales, book fairs, a drawing, etc.) and allocated for equipment. Be sure to plan ahead for easy-to-reach storage, too.

If children are wildly dashing around, they can learn some loosely-organized games. Children need supervised free play, but playing spontaneous games of four-square, hopscotch, and tether ball can fill many of the same needs in a safer fashion. If the students don't know the traditional games, help set up a way to teach them. A group of parents or retired teachers might be willing to donate a couple lunchtimes on the playground.

❦ ❦ ❦ ❦ ❦ ❦ ❦

Q *On vacation, we stopped at a park with equipment that was partially broken. My kids fussed and screamed when I wouldn't let them go down the slide. My husband even thought I was too cautious, but I didn't feel it was safe.*

A Protecting our children from harm inevitably includes some unpopular decisions. Much to our children's dismay, I always prefer to err on the side of safety than popularity.

Perhaps the next time, simply stop the car in the parking lot and look over the area. If garbage cans are overflowing or there is concrete underneath equipment, don't even enter the playground.

❦ ❦ ❦ ❦ ❦ ❦ ❦

Q *An older child I don't know has been bothering and teasing kids in our neighborhood. Is it wrong that I've had my four year old come in the house when the troublemaker comes around?*

A No. We are responsible for the safety and well-being of our children. Sometimes removing your child from a potential problem situation is appropriate. Another alternative is to talk directly with the "troublemaker." He might appreciate the suggestion that he would have more fun playing with children his own age. Or, if you are directly supervising play that involves everyone, you can restate basic rules of fair play for everyone. Of course, if the situation doesn't improve, you can suggest that the older child find another place to play.

🍎 🍎 🍎 🍎 🍎 🍎 🍎

Q *A mother I know has the safety rule for her son, "You can do it as long as you don't get hurt." What do you think about that?*

A The parent is inviting trouble for herself and her son. "Do it as long as you don't get hurt" indicates the person has not maturely accepted that basic responsibility of providing a safe, loving environment.

Unfortunately, some parents have adopted this policy without the brazen openness of your friend.

When a parent allows a baby to sit on someone's lap in the car, instead of being safely buckled into a child restraint and car seat, the parent is saying, "You can do it as long as you don't get hurt."

When young children are left alone at home the parent is saying, "You can do it as long as you don't get hurt."

When a parent allows a young adult to drink liquor illegally, the parent is saying, "You can do it as long as you don't get hurt."

Parenting abuses are all around. Our job is to do the best job that we can.

🍎 🍎 🍎 🍎 🍎 🍎 🍎

Q *Is it normal for a child to be tired at the beginning of the school year?*

A Yes. The opening of school can be tiring and stressful for students (and parents) of any age. It takes some students three or four weeks to make the transition from summer to school. Answer these questions to identify other reasons for your child's behavior:

• Is she getting enough sleep? Although children vary widely in the amount of sleep they need, be certain that she is getting at least as much sleep as she normally needs.

• Is she sleeping soundly? Has she had bad dreams recently or awakened you more often for a drink of water? A sleep-deprived child might wake up frequently during the night. If so, she might need a calmer, longer pre-bedtime relaxation period.

• Is her schedule too full? A complete day of school in addition to extra activities might add stress. Even activities which seem simple, like stopping for groceries or a new pair of tennis shoes, might overload a child's day. If you're always running errands with her after school, cut back until your daughter is back to her usual self.

• Is she comfortable at school? Phone her teacher to find out how she has adjusted at school and whether or not the teacher also notices her tiredness. Discuss ways to reduce any stress.

• Has she had a check-up recently? Phone your pediatrician and ask if he wants to see her. There might be a physical reason for her tiredness.

Q Can my daughter get a healthy tan without damaging her skin?

A There's no such thing as a healthy tan. Medical practitioners stress that a suntan is simply a socially acceptable form of skin damage.

❧ ❧ ❧ ❧ ❧ ❧ ❧

Q *My son's dream job has been to be a lifeguard, but I'm concerned about the possibility of skin cancer with his being outside in the sun all summer.*

A Most lifeguard stations provide some type of shade, but he will still need to take precautions to prevent sun damage. These include gradual exposure to the sun; wearing a hat, sun glasses, and T-shirt; and the consistent use of sunscreen. Many pools also rotate schedules so the same guards do not work daily during the high-sun hours.

❧ ❧ ❧ ❧ ❧ ❧ ❧

Q *With all the hype about sunburn, why doesn't somebody warn parents about keeping kids' heads covered? My toddler got her scalp sunburned because her hair was so fine.*

A That's a good warning. Also, remember to use sunscreen on the tops of children's feet, tops of the ears, and noses. Make sure they wear shoes, because sand and concrete can be blistering hot. A visor or cap can help shield a child's eyes from the sometimes-hurtful glare of the sun. The best advice, though, is to stay out of the sun during midday, when solar rays are strongest.

❧ ❧ ❧ ❧ ❧ ❧ ❧

Q *Glasses were just prescribed for my fourth grader. How can I get him to wear them?*

*A*Usually when a child sees how much clearer the world looks, he'll wear the glasses without question. But peer pressure is already starting to influence good judgment at fourth grade. Alert your son's teacher, so the wearing of glasses can be positively reinforced at school. It's also helpful to casually note others who wear glasses: students at school, respected teachers, or other adults who are important in your child's life.

Ask your son if he has any questions about the glasses. Perhaps he is wondering if he can still play basketball, if he has to wear them to take a shower, or how he'll play right field in the glaring sun without flipping down sunglasses. Give him opportunities to ask questions and talk about his feelings.

Also ask the doctor if contact lenses will be a choice for your son in the future. Sometimes, just the possibility of that option helps the situation appear less bleak.

Chapter Nine

Activities

* Choosing activities
* Setting limits
* Which league?
* Too young for baseball?
* Sports important at seven?
* Limiting activities
* Managing multiple activities
* Funding activities
* Which fund-raisers?
* Door-to-door selling safe?
* Fair to sell at work?
* Carpooling
* Appropriate movies
* Video vs. television
* Repeating videos
* Missing out on board games?
* Choosing piano teacher
* Managing Saturday sitter
* Quality time
* Nothing time
* Wrong toys?
* Bad to be bored?
* Quitting okay?
* Support vs. pressure
* Cheering on shy child
* Sleepover
* One-track reading
* Horror stories
* Family devotions
* Mealtime prayers
* Eating together
* Finding time
* The "right" swing set
* Ball park embarrassment
* Nursing home visit
* Sheltered lives

❧ ❧ ❧ ❧ ❧ ❧ ❧

Q *Should we sign up a child for activities or wait until he shows a particular interest in something before signing him up?*

A The answer depends on your flexibility, your child's age and personality, and your objectives for your child. But whether you or your child leads, clarify how you want your child to benefit before signing him up for anything.

Some children show an early preference for certain activities. Even a young child can be influenced by peers, advertisements, role models, or his God-given talents. If your child shows a specific interest, identify a developmentally appropriate experience in that area.

When a child has identified special skills and interests by the end of the middle-school years, he begins the teenage years from a position of strength, because he has a niche in which he excels. If your child is hesitant to explore options, simply suggest some possibilities. Children are often more willing to participate when they attend with a friend. Clearly state that taking one six-week class doesn't imply a lifelong commitment. Often an initial class is relatively inexpensive and offered by a local school, YMCA, museum, or community organization.

❧ ❧ ❧ ❧ ❧ ❧ ❧

Q *If I sign up my son for every activity he'd like, I'd spend hours every day driving him to lessons, practices, and games. Should I set a limit?*

A Children like your son (and one of our daughters) can easily lead an entire family into schedule gridlock. These children tend to thrive on activity and social contact. However, because even these children can learn the importance of balance in life, you might want to set basic family guidelines.

For example, in our family, a child can only participate in one sport at a time. It's okay that basketball practices overlap with soccer games for a couple weeks in November, but our children can't sign up for indoor and outdoor soccer at the same time. Or, you might permit each child to choose one music, one sport, and one other activity.

We often think that the only way to encourage a child's special talent is to sign him up for many activities, but there are other ways as well. Order a gift subscription to a special-interest magazine. Take your child to professional events, concerts, or exhibits. Encourage him to learn and read about the activity and the people who have excelled in it. These varied activities provide enrichment and instruction about the same subject from many different viewpoints.

❧ ❧ ❧ ❧ ❧ ❧ ❧

Q How do I choose the sports league that is best for my daughter?

A First, ask yourself how your child can benefit. Then, discuss various options with your daughter. She may want to join a team where she already knows other players. That might be more important than choosing a league with a prestigious reputation or low fees.

If the options appear equal, answers to these questions will help you make a decision:

• What are the goals of the program? Determine if the league will help your child meet her goals.

• When and where are games and practices? Decide how these times will fit into your family schedule.

• What is the cost? Ask about uniforms, league and tournament fees, and transportation.

• What are the expectations of parents? Find out about fundraising, participating in carpools, providing snacks, assisting coaches.

• What are the expectations of team members? Ask about out-of-class practice time, absences, tardies, and withdrawal penalties.

❦ ❦ ❦ ❦ ❦ ❦ ❦

Q Is a six year old too young to play baseball?

A No, not if the program reflects the developmental levels of a six-year-old child. Look for these values in a program:

• Instruction is the major goal. Every child should play a minimum number of innings in each game, regardless of skill level. It can be devastating for a six year old to sit on the bench for a whole game.

• Children learn skills gradually. For example, children should move over a period of years from hitting a ball off a tee, to hitting a ball pitched by an adult or mechanical pitcher, to hitting a ball pitched by a teammate. Avoid leagues that rush this process.

• Every child is a winner. Many instructional leagues don't even keep score. This emphasizes fun and learning for the players and parents. This approach prevents a parent from asking a young child, "Who won?" and puts the proper focus on, "Did you have fun?" If there are playoffs, every team should participate.

❧ ❧ ❧ ❧ ❧ ❧ ❧

Q *Is it important for a child to be in sports when he's seven years old?*

A General benefits include experiencing team spirit, learning how to cooperate with others toward a shared goal, dealing with winning and losing, learning from a person who's not Mom or Dad, getting exercise, learning the importance of training, and identifying or increasing skills.

From a developmental standpoint, a child does not need to participate in sports. Through other activities, he can receive the same benefits listed above. Your child can be a winner, with or without a team uniform.

So I would encourage you to personalize that question to read, "Is it important for *my* seven-year-old child to be in sports?" You are the only one who can answer that question, because you are the expert on *your* child.

❧ ❧ ❧ ❧ ❧ ❧ ❧

Q *I feel as though I live in the car, taking my kids everywhere. How can I control their activities?*

A Family life researchers have found that "children's activities" are a major source of stress, beginning in the mid- to late-elementary school years. So you are experiencing a common phenomenon.

Families deal with the situation in a variety of ways. Some families limit the number of children's out-of-school activities. In these instances, parents either say "You can have two activities this year" or tell the children exactly which activities are manageable. For example, a parent might explain, "You can't do gymnastics this year because I can't work out a carpool. Swim team and flute lessons will work out fine."

For families that set few or no limits, carpooling becomes essential. These families often use a large master calendar, posted in a central location at home. Activities for each family member can be written with a different color pencil.

As you examine this issue, continue to ask these important questions: "What is best for my child? What is best for our family?"

❧ ❧ ❧ ❧ ❧ ❧ ❧

Q *My daughter blew up when I told her she should limit after-school activities. She said she's waited all her life to be in junior high and she wants to do everything.*

A Junior high is a new world. This is often the first time children can choose from a wide variety of school-based activities. There is also peer pressure to participate. However, junior high activities can be balanced to respect family priorities and individual needs. Here are two suggestions:

1. Gather information. Ask your daughter to list all desired activities, with the practice times, performances, games, etc. Once you see everything on paper, the schedule might not look as bad as it sounds.

For example, many sports are seasonal, with little overlap. Softball, basketball, and soccer might be scheduled for different months. Other activities, like chess club, might meet just one afternoon each month. School newspaper work might be done during school hours.

2. Discuss choices. Let your daughter actively participate in making the decisions. For example, you might offer to drive some-

where twice a week. If she wants to join activities that require transportation on extra days, she might need to make her own arrangements. You can provide support in various ways, perhaps by pairing up with another parent to drive one night and talking with the team coach about using a school bus or driving carpool for the second night.

🐾 🐾 🐾 🐾 🐾 🐾 🐾

Q *Why do I have to pay to watch my own son play basketball in the school gym? I take him to practice, drive him to games, and buy him the kind of shoes the coach wants, and then I have to pay to get into a game? It's crazy.*

A I agree. Unfortunately, as you've pointed out, we parents accept much of the burden for our children's extracurricular activities.

In the past, schools typically paid a league fee to cover costs for uniforms, transportation, referee, coach, etc. The complicated situation of school funding dictates what we see happening today.

There isn't an easy, inexpensive, or simple response to your concern. In some areas, corporate sponsors support specific teams or groups. For example, a local bank may sponsor the chess club or math team; a hardware store might sponsor the girls track team. In other geographic regions, school activities are dependent on funds raised through fund-raising activities.

Investigate creative alternatives with your school administrator. I, and many other parents, would be interested in how you solve this problem.

❧ ❧ ❧ ❧ ❧ ❧ ❧

Q How do I pick which fund-raisers to let my child do?

A Use these guidelines:
1. Participate when the learning potential is high for your child. For example, look for opportunities when he can learn to present himself and his product, take an order, follow through with delivery, and learn the importance of customer service and satisfaction.

2. Choose fund-raisers for activities that are most important to your child. For example, if he's really into Scouting, consider supporting that activity.

3. Choose fund-raisers that give a high percentage of return to your child's activity. For example, your child's sports team might get only twenty percent from candy sales, but your school might get forty percent from a magazine drive.

4. Use common sense; participate when you can truly use the product.

❧ ❧ ❧ ❧ ❧ ❧ ❧

Q My son is furious because I won't let him go door-to-door selling candy bars for school. It's not safe.

A A growing number of groups and schools are starting to include an "activity fee" as part of registration costs. This is intended to eliminate direct selling.

No child's position on a team or activity should be based on fund-raising abilities. Adult sponsors (and parents) have the responsibility to design fund-raisers that do not involve potentially dangerous situations.

Phone your son's school principal and share your concerns.

❧ ❧ ❧ ❧ ❧ ❧ ❧

Q *Is it fair for the parent to sell school fund-raising stuff at work when his child gets the credit?*

A When making this decision, ask basic questions: How will your child benefit? What will he learn?

If your child will clearly grow from your selling, get permission from your employer before telling your child, "I can take some to work," or "You can come to the office to sell after school on Friday." (Companies might have specific guidelines.)

Some co-workers appreciate the opportunity to support children's activities; others feel obligated and resent the intrusion. Determine how your fund-raising will be perceived in the workplace. Your solicitation at the place of employment should be very low-key, if you participate at all.

❧ ❧ ❧ ❧ ❧ ❧ ❧

Q *How can I make a carpool work?*

A Set some ground rules before you begin ride-sharing. Here are some guidelines to consider:

• If a driver cannot drive for any reason (sick kids, sick driver, or sick car), the driver must call the next day's driver no later than forty-five minutes before the first child is picked up.

• There is a time span for picking up kids from home. (For example, a driver can come between 12:50 and 1:00). If no one is home at the start time, the driver will leave, assuming that other arrangements have been made for the rider.

• Children with gear (school books, tennis rackets, swimsuits, and towels) must use a backpack or bag. All bags are to be stored in the trunk.

• Children must change out of wet swimsuits before they come into the car.

• Third graders and above may open and close car doors. Younger children may not.

• All passengers' seat belts must be buckled before the car will start.

• When dropping off a child, a driver doesn't pull away from the house until an adult has come to the door. (An open door doesn't necessarily mean an adult is home for the child.)

• If no one is home when a child is to be dropped off, the driver will not leave the child there, but will take the child to the driver's home.

❧ ❧ ❧ ❧ ❧ ❧ ❧

Q I am uncertain whether or not to take my daughter, who's four, to see a movie all her friends have seen.

A Your judgment, your knowledge of your child, your child's background of experiences and perceptions, and your level of parent-child communication are all factors that would influence a response. This is true when discussing a family-rated movie for a four year old or a scary film for a twelve year old.

Your child is an individual; how a film will affect your child might be totally different from how it will affect your neighbor's four year old.

Instead of continuing to debate this issue with a "Should I" or "Shouldn't I" approach, ask yourself, "How would my child be enriched, entertained, encouraged, or nurtured by seeing this movie?" Then combine your interpretation of printed film reviews with your answer to that important question about your child. By asking how your child will benefit, you will focus on the potential merit of this film or similar experiences in the future.

$ $ $ $ $ $ $

Q *Is watching videos as bad for kids as watching TV?*

A A video tape gives you direct control over what your children watch. It also offers flexibility: you can turn it off at any point and say, "We'll finish watching it later."
A television program promises freshness and excitement because no one knows what will appear. But when we turn on the television, our children are not just seeing carefully chosen programs but also commercials. Both kinds of programming can influence our children.

Remember that the television is a convenient and very seductive baby-sitter. We can easily fall into the trap of letting our children watch the screen more often than is good for them. Balance viewing with other activities.

$ $ $ $ $ $ $

Q *Does it hurt my kids to watch the same video over and over? They must have seen it at least twenty-five times.*

A Some children love the security of knowing exactly what's going to happen next. This can give them a wonderful sense of familiarity, especially if they were somewhat scared during the first showing. Children also know the story has a beginning, middle, and end, so they automatically learn about the story line.

Repeatedly viewing the same story is not necessarily bad for you, either. You are fully aware of what is on the screen. You can also probably predict the children's mood at the end of the show. You know, for example, some programs might stimulate aggressive responses. If children are allowed to watch those videos, immediately after the show, guide them outside to practice their karate kicks. After *Cinderella*, children might want to sit with glue and glitter to make a picture of Cinderella's ball gown.

Ask yourself two questions to determine if watching this much-loved video is part of a good pattern: Is the video having a positive influence? What would they be doing if they weren't watching that show again?

💥 💥 💥 💥 💥 💥 💥

Q Are my kids missing out by not playing the board games I played when I was growing up? If it's not on a screen, my kids won't play it.

A In many families, a screen and joystick have replaced a die and marker.

Some high-tech games can support academic skills, foster hand/eye coordination, and provide exercises in logic, reasoning and problem solving. That's all good.

Board games tend to promote communication and group problem solving, taking turns, and learning how to win and lose. That's all good, too.

Having both options really expands opportunities for growing and learning through all kinds of games.

Whether you're buying a board or electronic game, look for

the same qualities:
- Developmental appropriateness
- A high probability that your children will like it—for long-term use, children will only play what they like
- A sound financial investment
- Promotes values you want to emphasize with your children.

Q How do I find a good piano teacher?

A You can let your fingers do the walking to the phone book, but don't stop there. Not all piano teachers advertise, so you'll need to do additional searching.

Ask for recommendations from other parents, the music teacher at school, the church music director, a local music store, or anyone you know who plays a keyboard instrument. Gather this information:
- How long is a lesson? Do you recommend a lesson each week, year round?
- What is the cost of the lesson, books, and other materials?
- Where do you teach? My house? A studio?
- How long do you expect a child to practice each day?
- How do you handle make-up lessons?
- How often are recitals held? Where are they held? What is the cost?
- What proportion of the lesson is music theory? Scales and chords? Actual songs? Will there be a mixture of popular pieces as well as classical?
- What do you expect from the parent?

After gathering this information, narrow down the list. Then set up an appointment to observe a lesson for a child about the same age as your child. Ask yourself:

• Would this teacher be able to motivate and encourage my child?

• Would my child feel comfortable making mistakes in front of this teacher?

• Would my child find working with this teacher enjoyable as well as educational?

Your work will pay off when you find a teacher who will help your child learn to play and to love music.

❧ ❧ ❧ ❧ ❧ ❧ ❧

How do I tell my Saturday sitter, in a nice way, that she lets my kids watch too much television?

Change the Saturday pattern by making a schedule. Set up basic elements that you want every Saturday: for example, two hours of outdoor play, one of quiet time in rooms, etc. Then discuss possible activities with the caregiver and children. Encourage everyone to contribute ideas.

Invest some extra time and effort to make sure things will go well. For example, if you want your children to have time alone in their rooms, take them to the library to get books before Saturday. Then they won't say, "There's nothing to do by myself."

If you want to completely eliminate Saturday-morning cartoons, rent a video for use on Saturday. Videos also have a set end time.

Food preparation can add interesting variety. Look through your recipe box and select some very simple menu items your children can make with supervision. They can make their own lunch or, even better, the children and sitter can have supper waiting when you come home on Saturday night.

After the first day of the new plan, get feedback on each part of the day. Change and refine your Saturday program as needed.

❧ ❧ ❧ ❧ ❧ ❧ ❧

Q *I signed up to be a Girl Scout leader so I could spend quality time with my nine year old. I like it, but she hates scouting.*

A It's great you want to spend quality time with your child, but be realistic as you visualize your definition of "quality time." Quality time isn't something to turn off and on. The best quality time reflects a relationship that has been developed over a period of days, weeks, or years and involves shared experiences.

It might take a while before you develop the kind of time you idealize. It also sounds as though scouting might not be the vehicle to accomplish this right now. Look for other short-term experiences that you could share.

You and your daughter could gather information from a variety of sources. As you seek opportunities, remember you don't need to be together one hundred percent of the time. You could even continue to lead Scouts if she decides to stop.

Quality time can happen in the car, in a class, or at home. You might want to both sign up for a museum program or take a craft or cooking course. Make a joint decision about what to do.

Your daughter is moving into a time when peers are becoming increasingly important. Consider quality-time possibilities that involve one of your daughter's friends and her mom, too.

❧ ❧ ❧ ❧ ❧ ❧ ❧

Q *I've arranged to be home when my daughter comes home from school, but all she wants to do is watch television.*

A Children relax in various ways. It's possible television is "nothing time" for your daughter. If she watches a favorite program with content and characters you approve of, that half-hour might serve as her relaxing time.

Sometimes the quality time we seek with our children doesn't work out. We might have "scheduled" it mentally into our plan, but children have other ideas. Some children might not want to talk when they get home. If this is true for your daughter, respect her need for time alone. Then look for other times that will be better for talking and listening.

Never feel your presence is unimportant. The after-school hour might not be working out the way you intended, but you are sending an unspoken message, "I have arranged my schedule to be with you as much as possible. This is one of many ways I can tell you I love you and care about you." A parent who arranges after-school care can affirm parental concern using similar words to convey those same thoughts.

🍂 🍂 🍂 🍂 🍂 🍂 🍂

Q My daughter has tons of toys, but she doesn't play with many of them. Are my parents and I buying the wrong toys, or is something wrong with my girl?

A The most common reason toys are unused is that they are chosen for entertainment instead of high play value. To find out if this is the real problem, ask yourself these questions:

1. How many toys and games encourage my child to play creatively?

2. Is there more than one way to use each game or toy?

3. Which toys are not used?

4. How many toys and games require a second person? Does she often have a friend with whom to play?

5. How often during an average day do I play with my child?

The second most common reason that toys are not used is related directly to organization. Make sure games are easily accessible and clearly visible. Rotate toys and games regularly; store some in a closet, and every month put away toys she has been using and bring out some "new" items.

Also "weed" the toys twice a year. Remove anything that is broken. Then plan to sell or give away unnecessary items or toys she has outgrown. Some parents do this before Christmas and a child's birthday, so there is space on the shelves for gifts. Others host family garage sales in early spring and again in late fall; children often like to sell their unused toys so that they can purchase new ones.

☙ ☙ ☙ ☙ ☙ ☙ ☙

Q Is it so bad for kids to be "bored"?

A No. Every child needs the opportunity to be alone, play in unstructured ways, and manage leisure time wisely. Until the last few years, "down time" was seen as a normal (not necessarily negative) element of childhood. Today, play dates are scheduled in advance, and children barely have breathing space between gymnastics, flute lessons, and after-school care. As a result, moments that aren't filled with organized activities suddenly become defined as wasted time.

Two problems have emerged.

First, parents and children depend on what I call "techno-entertainment fixes" instead of creative use of leisure time. Instead of getting out the building blocks for ten minutes before supper, a parent might say to a child, "All right, you can play Nintendo until it's time to eat" or "Eric, you can watch television for a few min-utes." As a result, Eric gets into the pattern of being entertained instead of learning how to entertain himself.

The second problem is that many children don't know how to make decisions about leisure time. Children are so accustomed to depending on others for organizing their schedule, they don't know how to manage their own time.

The next time your child complains, "I'm bored," encourage him to consider creative solutions and practice sound time-man-agement techniques.

$$ \mathcal{S} \quad \mathcal{S} \quad \mathcal{S} \quad \mathcal{S} \quad \mathcal{S} \quad \mathcal{S} \quad \mathcal{S} $$

Q *My son joined the school band last year, but he doesn't like it. Should I let him quit?*

A Your son might have discovered that band isn't what he thought it was going to be. Or, he might have new interests. Or, his friends might also be telling their parents, "I want to quit." The list of reasons could go on and on.

First, see if it's the band he dislikes or something else: the direc-tor, where he sits, the music, practicing, his instrument, his folder partner, or anything related to band.

Then, take your child to a band concert. When a new music student plays simple, repetitive pieces that are boring even the first time, it's easy to lose enthusiasm. It might be helpful for your son to see what the future might include if he stays with it.

Discuss the problem. If your son doesn't think he'll ever enjoy playing in the band, help him look for other interests.

❧ ❧ ❧ ❧ ❧ ❧ ❧

Q *What do you think of a parent who yells for his boy to "get a hit, get a hit" at every single game?*

A It's great when a parent shows support. However, there is a difference between support and pressure.

A supportive parent encourages a child to do his best. The parent asks, "How can I help you?" The parent makes it perfectly clear, by actions and words, that the child will still be loved, regardless of his performance.

A child who is pressured might feel that he is loved for what he achieves and not because of who he is.

There are so many positive ways we can help a child put forth his best efforts that it just doesn't make sense to apply pressure.

❧ ❧ ❧ ❧ ❧ ❧ ❧

Q *At school ball games, all the parents cheer for their kids, but my daughter got mad the one time I yelled for her. I feel odd when I don't show support.*

A You show support by being there. The type of support you give will change through the years as your child grows up.

It's good that your daughter told you honestly what makes her feel most comfortable. I recommend that before an event, a parent specifically ask a child, "Will it help if I cheer for you?" Beginning in the junior high years, some children do not want to be singled out in any way. For example, our daughter who ran track in junior high liked to hear, "Go, Angie, go!" Our son, who played baseball at the same age, was embarrassed if I even clapped when he came up to bat.

If a game yell doesn't help your daughter, be a cheerleader after the game. Saying, "You had a great, level swing in the fifth inning," might be more encouraging than a loud cheer. A behind-the-scenes approach will help you support many of your child's attempts, not just her obvious successes.

❧ ❧ ❧ ❧ ❧ ❧ ❧

Is it bad that my son only reads sports stories?

No. It's great he enjoys reading.

If he's reading the backs of baseball cards, sporting magazines, the sports section of the newspaper, and sports cards collectors' books, he's also seeing a broad range of writing styles.

Soon, he might branch out into related areas—biographies of sports figures or broadcasters, for example—but that will happen naturally as he will be required to read in various categories for school assignments.

❧ ❧ ❧ ❧ ❧ ❧ ❧

There was a book fair at school, and my sixth-grade son wanted some books. He doesn't usually like to read, but he picked out five paperbacks. I was thrilled. When I got home and looked at the them, I was shocked. Every book is a horror story. One cover says, "Jingle bells, Santa kills." Another has a werewolf. I don't want to say "no" now that he finally found something to read, but I don't want him reading that trash.

The books you purchased represent today's version of the rather innocent mystery and intrigue stories that you and I read while we were growing up. But you're exactly right: the Hardy Boys and Nancy Drew didn't include the physical violence and elements of horror that are a major part of many preteen fiction titles.

Should you let him read the books? It seems logical to let him read what you already bought and he selected, but I would read at least one book, too, so you can discuss it. Ordinarily, reading a book aloud together at bedtime is a good habit to build, but the content of these books doesn't lend itself to that.

And regarding future purchases, I don't agree with some parents who justify purchasing this type of book by saying, "Well, at least my kid is reading." There is good reading material available that doesn't focus on fear and goose bumps.

Identify a certain interest or theme that appeals to your son. Preteen boys especially like things that have current appeal. Consider some of these suggestions:

- The Civil War, especially if you can attend a reenactment
- Sports and sports biographies
- Space exploration, popularized by the highly-publicized shuttle launches
- Castles, knights, and dragons
- Dinosaurs
- Movie-related and holiday books

Remember that when you buy your son a good book, it's a gift he can open again and again.

Q *Family devotions aren't working. I don't like my kids to groan when I pull out the book, but I also want them to know it's something we should do daily.*

A You've taken the first two steps toward meaningful devotions: you've made devotional time a priority, and you want to find a format that fits your family. Your question tells me that you already know devotions can bring families closer to God and each other when the material is relevant and the time frame appropriate.

I assume you are using a traditional approach that includes reading aloud a prayer, Scripture, and printed material to bridge the faith-life gap. That works well for some families. But because that doesn't match the needs of every family, consider various formats. Begin with the baseline goal: time that will spiritually strengthen you and your family. Then find materials that will help you meet this goal.

Visit your local Christian bookstore or church library. Ask your children to help you identify materials that fit into the category of "Christian family time." For example, you might consider listening to a single song on a CD every day and then discussing it. Or, make a list of movies to rent; many of these have study guides suitable for family use. Your children might find age-appropriate magazines to read and then share. You might choose games which focus on Christian values. Consider various options as you seek what works best for your family at this time.

Q My kids have gotten into a rut with prayers before meals. The prayers seem to have no meaning. What can we do?

A First, discuss the issue with your children. They will probably suggest ways to vary the format and increase their participation.

When our family gets into this situation, we use singing prayers for a few days. Ask your church music director or pastor for resources.

Some families use a circle format: each person around the table can contribute a sentence or two. Or, put a Bible, prayer book, or devotional book in a napkin holder on the kitchen table. Family members can select prayers (verses from the Psalms work well) from these resources.

Or begin a family prayer journal. Simply put a notebook on the kitchen table. While supper is being prepared, or after dinner each evening, family members can record something for which they are praying. Younger children can draw picture prayers. This is an easy way to personalize prayer in a meaningful way. Date the entries, and you will have a record of this aspect of your family journey with Jesus. Older children might like to page back through the book and note the ways in which God has answered the prayers.

❧ ❧ ❧ ❧ ❧ ❧ ❧

Q *We think eating dinner together as a family is very important, but our son is rebelling because it means he can't play basketball, which practices during the supper hour. Should we hold out for what we believe?*

A As our children grow up, we don't need to change our values, but the way in which we live out our values will be shaped by experiences and opportunities.

Bonding with family members through special events and everyday happenings is an important value. The time of day at which you gather will reflect the schedules of family members.

Bonding with peers becomes increasingly important as children move into preadolescence. They begin to have a strong need to find a niche with peers. Team sports allow kids to be considered part of the "group." If the school gym is booked with numerous activities, practices during breakfast or supper might be the only available time slots.

Try some flexible thinking while maintaining your core value. If your baseline value is spending time together, that can be done in a variety of places and in many different ways. For example, family time might be at the breakfast table or when you drive the children to school before you go to the office. This means your family time won't necessarily fit the Norman Rockwell image, with everyone gathered around the dinner table.

Activities don't need to pull apart families, and family priorities don't necessarily need to stifle a child as he goes out into the world.

🐛 🐛 🐛 🐛 🐛 🐛 🐛

Q How can I find enough time to do everything I want for my two boys?

A Many parents would agree with you that twenty-four hours a day doesn't seem like enough. Use time-management techniques and look for hidden moments. Here's how:

Search for time blocks on the calendar that are not "booked." Then, over the next few days, identify how you and your sons are currently using those minutes. With this information, you'll sort through what's important and prioritize your time.

In addition, make an effort to interact with your boys during those hide-and-seek moments that happen every day. I'm talking about the times you shop for shoes, go grocery shopping, drive carpool, etc. A widely reported need for "quality, not quantity" time has shifted our perspective to view incidental moments with our children as unimportant. I agree that all of us need to have those intense times of interaction, eye contact, and active listening with our children. But don't underestimate the value of casual, everyday conversation and companionship.

Another factor that might contribute to your particular problem with schedule gridlock could be hidden in your question. You said, "I don't have enough time to *do* everything I want for my kids." Some parents feel they should do things *for* children instead of *with* children. Use this opportunity to re-examine your household chores and routines. Even preschoolers can learn how to store toys and put dirty laundry in the hamper. Please don't think you must do everything for your children.

🍎 🍎 🍎 🍎 🍎 🍎 🍎

Q *How can I pick the "right" swing set? A friend bought an expensive play set her kids never use, and my neighbors bought a cheap one their kids love.*

A As you've observed, a play set doesn't need to be expensive, but it does need to be carefully chosen. Begin the decision-making process by determining the needs of your family.

Physically, young children need to build strength, develop flexibility, and practice balance. Socially, they grow through interaction and dramatic play. It's quite possible to get all of these benefits through outdoor equipment, so ask yourself, "How should my child benefit from a play set?" List learning and growing opportunities you want in your own backyard. Then identify what is needed now and what can be added in the future. Shop for equipment that matches your child's needs, your site, and the space.

The first pieces of outdoor equipment I purchased for our children aren't even included in most backyard play sets. I bought a sandbox and lid (so it would not become a cat litterbox) and a child-sized table with attached picnic benches. My children were having many large-muscle needs met on wheeled toys. The sand-box and table helped meet my children's needs for unstructured socialization and creative play.

If you decide to purchase a swing set, look for equipment with ladder-rung distances appropriate for your child, sling swings, and below-ground installation anchors. Reputable companies cover nuts and screws heads. Plan on an eight- to twelve-inch depth of pea gravel, mulch, or another surface that will "give" if your child falls. (Packed dirt is not a suitable surface for underneath swings or at the bottom of a slide.)

If possible, locate equipment out of the sun, away from bee-attracting plants and bushes, and within viewing distance of a favorite window for your easy supervision.

ɤ ɤ ɤ ɤ ɤ ɤ ɤ

Q When you pay for tickets to take three eleven-year-old boys to a baseball game, is it all right to take food from home, or would that be, as my son says, "embarrassing"?

A Preteens are very sensitive to appearances. Taking food might not be embarrassing for you or me, but it might be for an eleven year old. Also, because buying food at the sta-dium might be viewed as part of the fun, I would buy some food there and consider these other ways to cut costs:

• Allow him to invite two other boys instead of three.

• Give each boy a reasonable allowance for spending at the park. Regardless of what they think, kids don't need to eat some-thing different in each inning.

• Take a couple typical ballpark snacks (peanuts, popcorn, etc.)

to supplement food purchased during the game.

• Offer your son the opportunity to earn some baseball-food money by doing extra chores.

• When inviting the boys, you can be up-front with their parents. You might say, "We'll buy each boy a drink and a hot dog, but if your son thinks he'll want more to eat, he might want to bring some extra money."

❧ ❧ ❧ ❧ ❧ ❧ ❧

Q How old should my children be before I take them to visit my elderly aunt in a nursing home?

A Your children's ages aren't as important as their maturity level and your aunt's health. First, ask about the rules at the nursing home. Find out the minimum recommended age for visitors and where young visitors may go.

Then, ask if your aunt would enjoy seeing the children. On your next visit, share some photos so you can get a feeling about whether or not the visit would benefit her. Are some days better for her than others? Does she prefer a certain time of day? Involve her in the planning. Also, get a recommendation from a health-care professional who serves your aunt.

Finally, talk with your children. Discuss specific health issues that might become apparent during the visit. ("Aunt Emma doesn't hear well in her left ear. We'll sit on her right side, and we might need to speak a little louder than usual.") This is an ideal time to talk about aging and ways we can show Christian caring for older people. Listen attentively for any concerns. Don't force a visit if a child is hesitant. Instead, ask the child to draw a picture that you can take to your aunt.

Before you leave for the nursing home, ask the children to pack a bag with some crayons and paper. Then if they get restless, they'll keep occupied and be able to leave a colorful reminder with your aunt.

Be realistic about your expectations. Ten or fifteen minutes can result in wonderful memories.

❧ ❧ ❧ ❧ ❧ ❧ ❧

Q My children lead a pretty sheltered life, but I want to show them they can make a difference in this world. Would it shock them or be a good thing to volunteer with our church group monthly at a homeless shelter?

A As Christian parents, we have a responsibility to help our children practice the compassion Jesus talks about in Matthew 25:45. We can do that by taking fresh bread to a sick neighbor, helping a child search for a lost pet, or participating in a walk to raise funds for the hungry. Volunteering at a local shelter might be a good way for you and your children to put social ministry into action.

Before you go:

• You might want to volunteer there alone, or talk with parents who have taken their children. This will help you determine whether or not this site is a wise choice.

• Allow your children to decide individually whether or not they will participate. The spirit of volunteering is giving from the heart; volunteering can't be forced. A child might prefer to show compassion in other ways, and that's okay, too.

• Older children are oriented toward peers. Recruit a friend with similar-aged children to accompany you. This will give built-in friends with whom to share the experience.

• Prepare the children for what they will see, emphasizing the similarities to your everyday life. The differences, which will be obvious, will quite naturally come up in discussion after your volunteering.

school

* Registration
* Reasons to transfer
* Christian vs. public school
* Choosing a school
* How to home school
* Badgered to volunteer
* Room mom alternatives
* More than fair share
* Parent chaperone
* Take-home papers
* Coaching for IQ test
* Tell IQ?
* Spelling bees
* Losing contest
* Verbal tests
* CD-ROM reading
* Really teaching reading?
* Fund-raising deluge
* Surprise grade
* Special testing
* Teachers' strike
* Teacher talk
* Outgrowing recess?
* Bored gifted kids
* Homework hassles
* Reading with children
* Disappointing school
* Improving school
* School theft
* Talking about school
* Raising grades
* Television in classroom
* Field trips necessary?
* Saving school papers
* End of the line

🐦 🐦 🐦 🐦 🐦 🐦 🐦

Q How do I go about signing up my child to attend school?

A Registration procedures and timelines vary. Often, school registration for fall is held in the preceding spring. You will find the name of your local public school district on your property tax bill. Phone the school office to find out the specifics of kindergarten registration. Here are questions to ask:

1. What is the cut-off date for kindergarten? (Most states have a specific date, such as June 1, by which a child must be five years old to qualify for fall attendance.)

2. What do I need to bring? (Many schools require a *certified* copy of a birth certificate and proof of residency in the district. Others ask for emergency numbers and health records, although you may usually complete such file information at home and return it to the school. Some school districts have the teacher visit your home. If the school office schedules this visit, take along your family calendar when you register.)

3. What is the registration procedure? (Parents and children might be introduced to the teacher in a large-group, after-school meeting. In other schools, you will simply sign up in the office or at a table set up in the gym. In this case, if parents share what they learn with their children, the children won't be disappointed if they don't even see the classroom, meet their teacher, or see other five year olds.)

🐦 🐦 🐦 🐦 🐦 🐦 🐦

Q I have a six-year-old son from a previous marriage. He's happy at the local public school. My new wife wants him to transfer to a

Christian school. What would you advise?

A Because your child is doing well at the school and is happy in the environment, I would be reluctant to change schools unless there are clear reasons to do so. This would be a good time to look carefully at your home program for prayer, devotions and Bible reading, so that your son continues to develop as a child of God.

Q *I want my child to grow up as a Christian. Is it important for him to attend Christian school?*

A Let's begin with what we know: Christian parents have the responsibility to help children grow up with Jesus. They know an environment can support a specific set of values.

Some parents interpret these statements to mean that enrollment at a Christian school is an important aspect of spiritual nurture. Other God-fearing parents choose to home school so that they can provide direct religious education. Still other parents enroll their child in a public school, which might offer numerous opportunities for witnessing and evangelism.

Choose the school that is best for you and your child. Children grow as Christians both in and out of the classroom. Regardless of where your child attends school the Christian lifestyle you model at home will influence your child's spiritual development.

Q *I'm getting remarried and my son will change schools. We have the choice of public, Catholic, or private. My ex-wife says she doesn't care where my son goes to school, as he'll live with me. How do we go about picking a school?*

A You and your wife both bring personal preferences, experiences, and family traditions to this issue. You're considering the school question against a background loaded with experiences and feelings, so first identify your personal priorities regarding school choice.

Next, determine the role your son will play in the decision: Will he visit schools with you? Will he make the choice himself? Depending on the age of your son, he might have some preferences and/or feel his voice should be heard.

Then, begin to gather information. Interview administrators at each school to identify what the school offers you and your child. Read the school handbooks. Talk with parents from both schools. Ask for the schedule of parent-group events. Compare media centers. Walk around the playgrounds. Find out about special services, food service, community involvement, and before- and after-school care. Most of all, observe the way teachers and staff relate to children and communicate with them.

Also, compare hard data.

You will find a complete curriculum in the school office. Additional information usually available as part of the public record includes test scores, educational level of teachers, class size, and specific data compiled to meet your state's guidelines.

Finally, list the benefits and drawbacks of each school. You will probably determine that there will be trade-offs, strengths, and weaknesses in all educational settings. Your child will benefit in various ways from any school he attends.

❦ ❦ ❦ ❦ ❦ ❦ ❦

Q *How do I start home schooling?*

A Begin by listing your child's social, emotional, physical, and cognitive needs. Some parents also include the fifth developmental area, spiritual needs. Then honestly answer the question, "Can I meet those needs for my child, a minimum of five hours each day for 180 days, in basic subject requirements?"

If you answer "yes" to that question, also answer the following questions before you make the commitment to home school:

1. What is required in my state? In some areas, students must register with the local school superintendent. Requirements vary, so get the facts in writing.

2. What is the transition process back to the public system? Even if you intend to home school for many years, learn the procedures for student grade placement, testing, and evaluation.

3. How can the local public school contribute to my child's home-school curriculum? Some home-schooled students participate in sports, fine arts, or other academic and co-curricular areas. Other parents choose to totally home school. Identify all options.

4. Who is currently home schooling in my area? Veteran home-schooling parents are a wonderful resource. Attend at least one meeting of a local support group before you make a definite decision to home school.

5. Why do I want to home school? Some parents decide to home school as a reaction against a system, teacher, or school. Other parents want to offer their child a personalized learning environment or specific curriculum. Clarify your own reasons.

6. What are the financial commitments? Read catalogs and visit bookstores and school-supply outlets to help you draw up an

annual budget. Include field trip and excursion costs, reference and computer materials, and curriculum.

As with any decision regarding school choice, you will probably discover positives and negatives. Weigh the issues, then make a choice based on what you feel is best for you and your child.

🐚 🐚 🐚 🐚 🐚 🐚 🐚

Q *Why does the school keep badgering me to "come and staple papers" and volunteer in other ways?*

A Schools need help. These jobs need to be done by someone, and there are not enough paid workers to do them all. It's also true that children benefit directly when their parents show interest in their school life and become familiar with the school through volunteering. That's why teachers and administrators want you to be involved. But your point is well taken: parent involvement should be encouraged, not forced.

Whether or not you choose to volunteer, you can show interest in your child's life at school in many different ways. This is what really matters. You might add little notes in the lunch box, a morning note on the day of a big test, an offer to bake cookies for a Friday party. These all tell your child, "I am interested in your school world. I care about you."

When possible, try to participate in events that will directly affect your child and get you into the school, around teachers and other parents. Attending an open house or the PTA meeting when your child is performing in a play are priority times.

🍎 🍎 🍎 🍎 🍎 🍎 🍎

Q *I've always been very involved in my kids' school. But this year I feel guilty because I have a job and can't be a room mother.*

A Your children are fortunate to have a mom who is so concerned. There are many ways to be involved in school life, whether or not you are employed during the day.

Write a note to each child's teacher offering to help. Specify exactly what you can do and your time frame. Many teachers are willing to send home work that can be brought back to school several days later.

Make yourself available in the same way to your parent/teacher organization. The refreshment committee is a great place for employed parents. Baking things in advance and then taking goodies out of the freezer just in time for school events has always worked well for me. If you have phone time available during the day for local calls, offer to help check out prices for competitive bidding on various PTA projects. Or, offer to make phone calls during the evening to recruit committee members or other workers.

Look for other short-term projects that will demonstrate interest in your child's school and give you an opportunity for service.

🍎 🍎 🍎 🍎 🍎 🍎 🍎

Q *As a parent chaperone on a school trip, should I be expected to buy snacks for the kids in my group?*

A No. Usually, teachers or caregivers provide a simple list of guidelines for adults who participate in a class activity.

Such suggestions normally include, "You are welcome to bring younger children to our plays and musical performances, but we are not equipped to handle siblings on trips," and "Parents may not purchase souvenirs, food, or anything else for one, more, or all of the children during the excursion."

Reminders like these ensure that your attention is focused on the students in your care and that children in all groups are treated equally.

❧ ❧ ❧ ❧ ❧ ❧ ❧

Q My older children always brought home papers from school, but the youngest hardly ever brings home papers. Why?

A There are usually two reasons parents don't see school papers: your child doesn't show you what he gets at school, or reduced amounts of paperwork are being sent home.

If your son remembers getting papers, ask him to check his backpack. Then, ask if his desk is cleaned out. It's amazing how much can be squashed into lockers, too. Identify a place right now where he will put all papers as soon as he comes home. For example, you might set an empty shoe box on the dining room table: all school papers should be put there immediately after school.

But your son might not have received many papers. Because important papers have ended up on school buses and driveways, school personnel now mail newsletters, registration forms, and other important information.

Also, classroom learning doesn't necessarily involve paper and pencil. The equation we used for so long, "many papers from school = children are learning a lot," just isn't true. For example, instead of completing a workbook page, your son might demonstrate knowledge by putting together a skit or working on a computer.

And with increased sensitivity to environmental concerns, school personnel have made a real effort to reduce the paper blizzard.

But if you're still concerned, talk with your son's teacher.

Q *What's the best way to coach my son before the next IQ test?*

A The educational goal for you as a parent is to help your son develop skills and abilities. Focus on the needs of your child as a learner instead of your ego needs as "parent of a gifted boy."

We all like our children to excel, but getting into a specific class might not be the best way to meet your son's educational needs at this time. Five years from now it might not matter whether or not your child was in the gifted track, but it will make a difference if he knows how to communicate clearly, feels good about the person he's becoming, and has learned skills that will translate into a steady job. Focus on helping him in these areas.

Support his ongoing class work. Give positive feedback. Host meetings where he and his friends can work on class projects. "Coach" your son in a life-long approach to learning by taking him to museums, discussing the news, and modeling community service.

And make sure he begins the test day just as he begins every other school day: with a good, restful night's sleep and a nutritious breakfast.

🌿 🌿 🌿 🌿 🌿 🌿 🌿

Q *Should I tell my child his IQ score?*

A No. In most cases, I don't believe that knowing an IQ score benefits either a child or parent. There is also a significant risk of such data being misinterpreted and misunderstood.

When properly interpreted and analyzed, results from an IQ test may help a professional design individual learning programs or give data useful in clinical assessment situations.

But would knowing your child's IQ help you parent more effectively today? Would knowing his IQ benefit your son tomorrow?

As a parent, knowing the results of other tests is far more useful. For example, if your son is left-brained, he will memorize more easily when he takes time to clearly organize school material. If he is a visual learner, it probably won't help to listen to a cassette tape of questions and answers before a history test. It will help him write out answers to questions.

This is the kind of test data that your child can use to understand himself and you can use to parent more effectively.

🌿 🌿 🌿 🌿 🌿 🌿 🌿

Q *Are you for or against spelling bees?*

A When a spelling bee showcases student achievements and awards excellence, I'm all for it. But when a spelling bee or any other academic contest is set up in a way that skews the field or adds unnecessary pressure, I'm against it.

Some schools use a team approach for spelldowns in the lower grades. This is a natural way to introduce younger students to academic competition.

As students move through school, teachers might prepare students for a spelling bee by adding "challenge words" or extra vocabulary words that are written regularly on the chalkboard. Other teachers add new words—from science, geography, or history—as they are used in class discussions. When extra credit words are used in a spelling bee, students are encouraged to go beyond the basic expectations. These are spelling bee-related activities that urge students to reach for excellence, examples that I applaud.

🐌 🐌 🐌 🐌 🐌 🐌 🐌

Q *How should I have helped my son when he was upset after being eliminated from the school geography bee?*

A Supporting students as they deal with the painful side of competition requires many parenting skills. We can listen as our children complain. We can give a hug when they cry. And when they say, "It wasn't fair," we can agree that "life isn't fair."

If your son joined you in the audience after leaving the stage, squeezing his hand to remind him of your love and support was probably best. You might also tell him specifically why you were proud of him—"You represented the whole fourth grade."

When a child is disappointed in his performance, avoid saying, "It doesn't matter." The loss does matter to him.

Also, don't rush the learning process. At some point in the future you can help him see that this event was just one of many contests in which he'll participate, but right now, avoid launching into a big lecture.

Be alert to clues for conversation that your son will give you over the next few days and weeks. Then this event will become a real learning experience for your son, because you'll meet his needs right where he's at. Later, you might discuss winning, losing, disappointment, expectations, and pride, but this opportunity might still come in the distant future.

🍂 🍂 🍂 🍂 🍂 🍂 🍂

Q My daughter's teacher reads a test question and then gives time for kids to write the answer. This is the first year my girl has had tests, but she has to see a question to answer it. What can I do?

A Some children receive information most easily using their ears; others depend more on their eyes. By writing down questions, students who are visually oriented do fine. Those who work best using their ears can read the questions to themselves. A written test also offers students the opportunity to self-pace the work, spending more time on some questions than others. That's why written tests are most common.

Explain the problem to the teacher. School personnel might suggest a learning-style assessment that would give valuable information about your daughter.

🍂 🍂 🍂 🍂 🍂 🍂 🍂

Q Will kids learn to read faster using a CD-ROM than a book?

A Until researchers have the opportunity to study the issue over a long period of time, I'm not sure anyone will know the answer to that question. I still suggest that one of the best things you can tell your child is, "Get a book. Let's read."

❧ ❧ ❧ ❧ ❧ ❧ ❧

Q *How can I tell if the school is doing a good job teaching my son to read?*

A Walk by your son's classroom. Do you see stories hanging up that children have dictated or written themselves? If you see a lot of child-related writing, the chances are great that reading is supported in his first grade.

Find out, too, how much time is spent in language arts. Many primary-level students write stories in science and record measurements in math that relate to reading throughout the day. These activities are designed to not only help children grow as readers, but also to help children grow up with a love of reading.

And there's the key element: if your son likes to read now, he is on the right track to become a lifelong lover of books.

❧ ❧ ❧ ❧ ❧ ❧ ❧

Q *I have only one child in school, but her band sold candy bars, her soccer team sold pizza, the school sold candy and had a read-a-thon, and her scout troop sold wrapping paper. I'm fed up with spending money on junk.*

A A school administrator has the responsibility to oversee all school-related fund-raising. Most administrators use a master plan to avoid the situation you describe. In an increasing number of schools, clubs are encouraged to limit the number of fund-raising activities during a school year or are required to follow guidelines. However, even if school fund-raisers are limited, church and community fund-raising efforts often overlap.

Fund-raisers have a high irritation factor for parents and other community members. I disagree with educators and elected officials who say that family-intrusive fund-raising is a fact of life. There are numerous types of optional, out-of-school fund-raisers that are nonthreatening to families: a food co-op, bicycle clinic, silent auction, parent/teacher talent show, parents' night out, etc.

Address your concerns in a letter to your school administrator. Also take an active role in the organizations that are raising funds. This will give you direct input into decisions. Parents like you who care deeply about issues like this can make a difference.

❧ ❧ ❧ ❧ ❧ ❧ ❧

Q *The first-grade teacher told me my son was doing great, but he got a B in math on his report card. Why would she have told me everything was fine when he only got a B?*

A You've pointed out a key problem with assigning letter grades to primary-age students: grades only tell part of the school story. For example, your son might work well with others, be an attentive listener, or follow classroom rules, but those important life skills won't be recorded. That's precisely why many primary-grade teachers use a variety of narrative or short-response forms to record that progress.

Ideally, student development is tracked in a portfolio, which is simply a collection of work. This not only showcases the new skills a student has learned, but reflects individual developmental differences and gives a more accurate assessment, because the child is compared to himself, not to others.

Ask your son's teacher about ways in which you can help your son in math, but please don't push him. First-grade boys typically vary widely in academic achievement.

Also, don't panic. A single letter on a first-grade report card does not indicate your son's potential or his future. The grade reflects progress in only one academic area as reported over a brief period of time.

🐛 🐛 🐛 🐛 🐛 🐛 🐛

Q My son's teacher recommended testing to find out why he's having trouble learning to read. I don't think anything's wrong with him, but on the other hand, I don't want him to keep having trouble. What should I do?

A Request testing as soon as possible. It can be painful to hear that something might be wrong. It's very tough to separate our reputation as a parent and dreams for our child from actions that will help our child. Be honest with your feelings, but then ask yourself, "What is best for my child?" If he's already faced disappointment at school, testing could identify the problems and offer some solutions.

Once I get beyond my personal ego hurts as a mom, I am usually grateful for test results, a teacher's guidance, or any other credible information that will benefit my child. Perhaps you'll feel the same way.

🐛 🐛 🐛 🐛 🐛 🐛 🐛

Q Can students legally attend school during a teachers' strike?

A Yes, if the county superintendent of schools ensures that certified teachers staff the classrooms. However, this often presents an awkward situation, because it can be difficult to find qualified teachers. For example, a math teacher could end up in an art class. The person is certified to teach, but not necessarily qualified to teach art.

❧ ❧ ❧ ❧ ❧ ❧ ❧

Q I was so upset when the teacher called about a problem with my son that when I got off the phone I couldn't remember exactly what she said. Do I call her back?

A Yes, and this time, take notes.
At the beginning of any conversation with a teacher, doctor, or other professional who works with your child, ask if you can get pencil and paper. Then write down what the person says. You might need to refer to these notes later, so write down as specifically as possible what the person says instead of your own feelings or responses. Date your notes and file them in an appropriate folder (under health records, school, soccer, etc.).

❧ ❧ ❧ ❧ ❧ ❧ ❧

Q When do kids outgrow recess?

A We never outgrow our need for relaxation through unstructured time.
Children need some unstructured time. Traditionally, it has come during the school day at recess, but it doesn't need to happen then. "Nothing time" can occur while waiting for the morning bus, during lunchtime, or after school.

Historically, recess provided a break in the classroom routine. This was necessary when children sat on benches for long hours in dimly lit classrooms. Today, our students are involved in learning-center activities, experiments, and a variety of hands-on experiences that provide physical as well as mental activity.

Remnants of outdoor education, which was a major thrust in the 1970s, resulted in a lasting legacy in which school grounds are viewed as a learning laboratory. When education isn't confined to a single classroom, children don't have as strong a need to "get out and run around" at recess. Variety of place, movement, and participation is built into the school day. Many teachers allow students, within reason, to use the bathroom whenever necessary, so a scheduled bathroom break isn't needed either.

Although the reasons for recess have decreased, many schools still schedule a midmorning break for primary-aged children, simply because young children learn so much through play. Often, though, scheduling recess at any grade level is an option of the local school board.

🍏 🍏 🍏 🍏 🍏 🍏 🍏

Q Why do schools bore gifted kids, like my son, by teaching them what they've already known for years?

A You are right: teacher training and state funding are often targeted to remediation instead of enrichment and advancement.

Talk with your child's teacher or administrator. Work with them to identify learning goals for your child. Clarify ways you can support his learning.

When you approach the school with a willingness to assist and an open attitude, you will be a great asset to your son.

❧ ❧ ❧ ❧ ❧ ❧ ❧

Q *I get upset and yell, and my kids still don't get their homework done. What's wrong?*

A As you've obviously learned, yelling seldom helps the homework situation. So begin with the basics. Be certain your children are bringing home the correct assignments. Get them a little notebook, and tie on a pencil so they can write down every assignment as it is given.

Then look at where your children generally work. There should be no distractions, so turn off the television, video game, and computer.

Also look at when your children work. Be sure they are "fed and watered" so "I'm hungry" doesn't interfere.

Help your children clarify and organize their work. Ask your children to check off in their assignment books each task as it's completed. A lack of good organization frequently contributes to homework problems.

Be alert to your children's skills. Can they put down their thoughts and ideas in writing? Do they really understand the material? If you observe something unusual, talk to the teacher immediately. As a parent, you can often discover little aspects about your child that dramatically affect learning.

Be consistent with homework rules. For example, you might say, "You may make or accept phone calls only after homework is finished."

If your children still don't finish their homework, there might be too many assignments. Talk with the teacher.

🍎 🍎 🍎 🍎 🍎 🍎 🍎

Q *The teacher said I should read with my son every night, but it's a struggle because he's so slow. How can I make it easier?*

A "Read with your child" probably means two things: let your child read to you, and you read to your child. Check with your son's teacher, though, to clarify the assignment.

First, choose a time when you and your son feel the most relaxed. Right after supper is often a good time. Just before bedtime will work only if he's not too tired.

Next, make sure your child is comfortable. Sit in front of a table or where the book will lie flat. Give your child a bookmark or index card to use as a marker above each line of type.

Finally, remove all distractions. Turn off the television and put out the dog. Learning to read requires intense concentration.

This "almost reading" stage is similar to that of "almost toilet trained"—all those trips to the bathroom take more time than just changing a diaper. Listening to an early reader and reading to an early reader take more time than if you read the book alone. But every time you read with your son, you support his newly learned skills.

🍎 🍎 🍎 🍎 🍎 🍎 🍎

Q *We moved to this school district because it had the best schools, but now that the kids are in the school, I've learned this district is not really very good.*

A I can sense your disappointment. It's time to make the best of a difficult situation.

First, list good and not-so-good points about the school. Sometimes when we feel generally negative, it's easy to forget the positives.

Next, note the negatives that directly influence your children's school experience. Then identify the avenues or people responsible for each individual item. Now select a doable job: isolate a specific task with a goal you feel can be achieved.

Informally scout around for board members, parents, and teachers who might share your ideas. Working as part of a larger group is very effective. In a school community, there really *is* strength in numbers.

The PTA—or whatever the parent organization is titled—is often overlooked as an ally for school improvement. This group is usually set up to help children get the best possible education. Whenever possible, use parent groups or school boards that are already in place. The leaders have a history of the situation, understand the power situations, and have the connections to get things accomplished.

Work as a team member for the good of all children, and you'll gradually see improvement.

❧ ❧ ❧ ❧ ❧ ❧ ❧

Q *What is the fastest way for me to improve my child's school?*

A Be actively involved. Offer to sponsor a club or school team. Show your support, not just your dissatisfaction. Run for office in the parent group or school board. Talk to your district officials and school board members.

When you perceive a problem, offer several solutions. Clearly state your willingness to help. Also listen. Sometimes it's easier to rant and rave than hear other points of view. Deal honestly with people. If this sounds too simple, it is. It's just that too often the basics of open communication are forgotten when our children's well-being is involved.

Don't set up the school as the enemy. Remember that you and your child's teachers, administrator, and board members are all working toward the same goal: to help children learn. When people become crusaders, they tend to forget that the best home/school relationship is a partnership.

❦ ❦ ❦ ❦ ❦ ❦ ❦

Q *Last year, my son had so many things stolen at school that I hate to spend money buying school supplies this year. Is there any way to protect his things?*

A You probably worked closely with the classroom teacher and school administrator last year. Make a friendly phone call now to ask the principal about ways security has been improved. Also find out how respect for property and problem-solving techniques are integrated into your child's classroom curriculum.

Here are three additional points:

1. Be certain your child pays attention to personal belongings. This is the best defense against loss.

2. Attach permanent labels to everything, including items you think might never get lost, like gym shoes.

3. Ask your son to take to school only what is absolutely needed. Many students carry unnecessary items in their backpacks.

❧ ❧ ❧ ❧ ❧ ❧ ❧

Q *How can I get my son to tell me about what happens at school?*

A Some children provide a detailed account of the day without any prodding. Other children need specific questions to recall the details. Still others feel school is their "territory" and don't wish to share much at all. What pattern fits your child? Base your expectations on knowledge of your child, not on how much the neighbor child talks about school.

For some children, straight "talking" time with a parent isn't fun. Other children warm up to the topic when asked direct questions. (Who did show and tell today? What did she bring in? What was the book about that you read in group time today? Did you get a turn in the loft today?)

Teachers want to help. That's why students come home with materials to be signed by an adult, simply so parents have some knowledge of what happens in the classroom. In other schools, parents are asked to write brief journal entries each night or once a week to guarantee some home/school interaction.

Remember that quality time doesn't need to be limited to pure talk. Great talks can happen when both of you are "trapped" in the car. And some of the most valuable time with children involves conversation plus activity. For example, playing catch with your son after school might help him relax so he feels comfortable talking about his day.

Find a comfortable niche between being nosy and expressing interest about school. Don't push your child so hard to talk about a spelling test or social studies project that he resists telling you about really important things. What matters is that your child knows you support him at school, you are interested in what he does at school, and you are willing to listen to whatever he will tell you about his day.

🍎 🍎 🍎 🍎 🍎 🍎 🍎

Q *The teacher said my son could get better grades, but how should he do that?*

A That's an excellent question to ask the teacher. Get specific information. Ask questions like these:
• Does my son seem to understand what you present and what he reads?
• Do the grades accurately reflect his achievement?
• Does he have effective work habits in the classroom?
• Does he organize his work time well and use leisure time constructively?
• How often does he volunteer answers?
• Is he a leader or follower in small-group projects?

Get a good description of your child at school from the teacher. Then focus specifically on strengths and problem areas. Set a time, perhaps in two weeks, when you and the teacher will talk again to evaluate the progress.

🍎 🍎 🍎 🍎 🍎 🍎 🍎

Q *How much TV should kids watch at school?*

A A video is a supplementary classroom aid. In most cases, students learn by experience, not by watching images. Videos or movies can introduce students to a topic or provide experiences that can't be duplicated in a classroom. Videos should be carefully selected to help meet instructional goals.

Talk to your child's teacher or the school administrator if you feel your child is watching too many videos or inappropriate movies.

❦ ❦ ❦ ❦ ❦ ❦ ❦

Q *What good are field trips? The kids have fun on the bus, eat lunch outside, and don't learn a thing.*

A Field trips are planned by a teacher to help meet learning goals for a specific unit of study. As an example, second graders might visit a bank to learn about the "real" world of money, or fourth graders might visit the state capitol to observe a session of the legislature. Appropriate classroom activities help prepare students for the trip.

Students should benefit from such field experiences by gaining confidence in a new learning environment and using "school" skills in a real-life situation.

If you wonder what your child has learned from a recent field trip, ask the teacher.

❦ ❦ ❦ ❦ ❦ ❦ ❦

Q *How do I decide which school papers to save and which ones to throw away?*

A Here are some guidelines:
• Save all formal records: report cards, grade sheets, health records, school newspaper articles written by your child or that mention your child, and notes from teachers. I recommend you save all communication from a teacher while your child is in that class. After the term ends, save just the notes with special meaning.

• Save items that are "firsts": the first time she prints her whole name, the first "I'm proud of you" note that comes from the teacher, the label from her first coat hook or cubby. These become "landmark" symbols that you'll enjoy seeing again in years to come.

• Save unique holiday items that store flat. Eliminate those that use food, are hard to store, or are extremely fragile. For example, don't save a gelatin painting or a three-dimensional paper sculpture. The one exception is artistic work you might use in holiday decorating, such as Christmas tree ornaments.

• Save items that demonstrate your child's special talents and uniqueness. She might paint a snowman with "personality" or draw a picture of "What I'm going to do when I grow up." Before you pack away a key piece of work, take a photograph of your child holding the work.

• Save items which might bring a smile—for you and your child five years from now.

• If you intend to frame anything, do it now, when the paper is in good condition.

• Date everything.

• If you have more than one child, write your child's name on everything. It's tempting to think, "I'll always remember who did that," but label everything just to be sure.

• Store in your memory box those special cards that say "I love you." Your child's "stuff" will become memories for you, too.

Q *Our last name begins with W and my son is always last in line. It's a little point, but it really bothers him. Should I talk to the teacher?*

A Yes, but it would be better if your son talked to the teacher. It's very important that children learn that talking with a teacher is a good thing. Your son also needs to know the importance of sharing his feelings in an appropriate way about something that is important to him. If he needs your physical support, stop by some morning before school to stand there while he talks with the teacher.

Lining up children by those who are wearing stripes, by the last letter of their first name, or by those who ate oatmeal for breakfast are ways teachers encourage attentive listening. Your son's teacher will probably appreciate a gentle reminder of how it feels to always be last in line.

seasonal

Fall
* First-day stress
* Nonviolent costumes
* School observation
* Thanksgiving activities
* Blended Thanksgiving

Winter
* Beyond snowball fights
* Christmas greed
* Christmas tree conflict
* Best gifts
* Photo with Santa
* Outgrowing Christmas
* Holiday baking
* After-Christmas boredom
* Teacher thank-yous

Spring
* Easter-egg hunt pagan?
* Easter candy alternatives

Summer
* Prioritizing events
* End-of-school whine
* Cutting hotel costs
* No playmates
* First-time camper
* County Fair
* Fourth-of-July disaster
* Picnic activities
* Sharing car-trip chores
* Backseat battleground
* "Tourist junk" alternatives
* No summer trip
* Children's choices

🦋 🦋 🦋 🦋 🦋 🦋 🦋

Q How can I help my son avoid being so stressed on the first days of the school year?

A Here are some ways to reduce your son's stress:
• Boost your child's social confidence. Encourage your child to phone a classmate or to invite a friend to lunch before school even opens. Or, help your child make arrangements to meet a friend on the playground when he arrives at school the first day. One of the most common fears for a child is that he'll be alone or that "no one will like me." Knowing he can walk into school with a friend eliminates a potentially major concern.

• Listen as your child talks about the coming year. Encourage him to share feelings and concerns. Even if he is "just" beginning a new grade in the same school he attended previously, a child can feel a little scared.

• Establish a nightly routine. After a summer of relaxed bed-times, gradually introduce the nightly routine you will enforce during the school year. This includes setting an appropriate time for "lights out." If your son usually selects his clothes for the next day or reads before going to bed during the school year, start those routines about a week before school begins.

• Establish a morning routine. Many families typically suffer stress during the "rush hour" of the first few school mornings. Prevent this by the same kind of advance preparation you use at night. If your child is required to walk the dog, take out the trash, or make his bed before catching the school bus, set that pattern now.

• Help him feel prepared. Complete all medical and emergency forms. Use the supply list from school to make sure your son has the materials he will need. Help him choose a backpack or clean out last year's lunch box. Just being physically ready can help a child feel emotionally prepared to face school.

🍎 🍎 🍎 🍎 🍎 🍎 🍎

Q *What are some nonviolent Halloween costumes for boys?*

A Costume options for both boys and girls include:
 • Occupations—such as carpenter, painter, doctor, dentist, office employee, police officer, firefighter, artist.
 • Entertainers—clown, singing star, figure skater, ballet dancer, puppeteer, acrobat.
 • Sports figures—tennis player, baseball player, figure skater, Olympic medal winner.
 • Historical figures—George Washington Carver, Clara Barton, Abraham Lincoln, Queen Esther, Johnny Appleseed.
 • Animals—including those from a favorite book, such as Babar the Elephant, Paddington Bear, Curious George, Clifford the Big Red Dog.
 • Inanimate objects—toothbrush, toothpaste, portrait in frame, salt shaker, candy bar, playing card, sandwich, goldfish in bowl.

🍎 🍎 🍎 🍎 🍎 🍎 🍎

Q *My son's school invited parents to "observe" classes during a special week, but I don't know what to observe.*

A Schools typically open their doors to parents and guests during National Education Week each November. This is a wonderful opportunity to learn more about your child's world at school.

You will probably sign in at the office and be given a nametag. This is a standard security procedure. Then you will be told where to find your student. When you enter the classroom, you might find adult-sized chairs available for guests.

Watch how your child relates to peers, responds to the teacher, follows instructions, organizes his materials, and participates in the class discussion. For example, ask yourself, "When the teacher is talking, is my son looking at the teacher, scrounging around in his desk, or playing with his pencil?" or "When the students split up into groups, did my child know where to go, take materials he needed, and talk easily with other students?"

Look around the room for evidence of his work; that will give you something to discuss with him. Jot down positive comments, questions, and concerns.

After the visit, leave a note in the teacher's mailbox if you'd like a conference. Write suggested times and a phone number at which you can be reached.

Q *In about the middle of the afternoon on every Thanksgiving Day, my kids complain they are bored, even though there are cousins running all over the place. Do you have any suggestions?*

A Think through the day's schedule from your children's perspective. Plan ahead to meet basic needs with activities and supervision.

• Even though it's a holiday, your children's stomachs will still be on regular time. If the "big dinner" is scheduled around a late football game, plan a snack for the usual mealtime.

• Take along a football or Frisbee so children can release pent-up energy.

• Ask children to collect nature items on a walk around the neighborhood: pine cones, buckeyes, acorns, etc. If the items are placed inside a cardboard box, an adult can spray paint them gold or silver. Children can add thread or nylon fishing line for hangers and give one to each adult as a Christmas ornament. Or, they can make them into mobiles attached to twigs.

• Have children write a *Thankful Times* newspaper. Children can ask Thanksgiving guests to tell the five things for which they're most thankful. Then the children can write up and illustrate the interviews. Photocopies of the newspaper can be made another day and mailed to the families who attended and to loved ones who could not attend.

• Suggest children plan a play about the First Thanksgiving to present after dinner. Limit costumes and props to things they can make out of construction paper.

• Ask children to decorate placecards, nut cups, or placemats for the Thanksgiving table.

Make arrangements, in advance, for a teenager or other adult to supervise the children. On holidays, there are typically a lot of adults around, but except for the babies whom everyone wants to hold, children are often left to float. That's when children not only get bored, but get into trouble.

🍎 🍎 🍎 🍎 🍎 🍎 🍎

Q How can we make sure Thanksgiving Day will go smoothly for our newly "blended" family?

A Identify traditions that each person brings with him. Look for ways you can incorporate as many traditions as possible. Some traditions can probably be changed or adapted just a little to meet the new needs of the family, and the person will still feel a positive tie to his past.

Because you are starting a new family group, also begin at least one new tradition. For example, you might draw names for a Christmas gift exchange or start the first page of a Thanksgiving memory book, in which people can record each year the blessings for which they are most grateful.

🎵 🎵 🎵 🎵 🎵 🎵 🎵

Q *What else can kids do in the snow besides have a snowball fight and make snowmen?*

A They can make castles, complete with towers and bridges. Save plastic margarine containers. These are great for molding snow. Snow packed into funnels makes turrets.

Or, challenge your children to make different kinds of tracks using just a shovel. They can use a snow shovel or a plastic shovel from the sandbox.

Check out a book on animal tracks from the library. Copy the pages with animals prints so you can go track-hunting with the children.

For a tasty treat, have the children scrape off the top layer of snow to reach the clean, white stuff. Collect a bowl full of snow, and top with pancake syrup.

And if you have room in the freezer, make a few snowballs to bring out next summer.

🎵 🎵 🎵 🎵 🎵 🎵 🎵

Q *My son can't wait for the Sunday paper so he can look through the Christmas ads and find what he wants. How can I help him see that Christmas is more than "getting"?*

A Move the focus away from him with these suggestions:
• Involve him in the giving. A child can decorate cookies, assist with wrapping, and help deliver gifts. We often expect our children will just "catch" the joy of giving. We need to plan their involvement so they personally experience that joy.

• Encourage participation in activities that benefit others. Most school classes, Scout troops, and clubs sponsor food drives or other events to support the less fortunate.

• Model the joy you feel in giving. Our children quickly perceive our joy—or our frustration—during the busy days before Christmas.

• When the next Sunday paper arrives, hand your child a marker or crayon. Ask him to circle pictures in the advertisements of items he thinks would make good gifts for *other* family members. Then refer to his suggestions when you shop.

❦ ❦ ❦ ❦ ❦ ❦ ❦

Q *My husband thinks putting up a Christmas tree is blasphemous. Even though our children are little, they love the lights and ornaments, and I don't see anything wrong with it. Who's right?*

A The origin of the Christmas tree is unknown. Some sources refer to a legend with Saint Boniface of Crediton. Other references credit sixteenth-century reformer Martin Luther. We do know that the Christmas tree isn't mentioned in the Bible.

On Christmas we celebrate the birth of Jesus. Christians typically have many customs which point toward this real meaning of Christmas. It's true that cluttering up Jesus' birthday by focusing on football games and presents can detract from the real meaning of the season.

In our family, we light candles on an Advent wreath during the four weeks before Christmas. Creche figures march through the house toward the manger in the days before Christmas. We have a birthday cake for Jesus, complete with candles, on December 25. Our Christmas tree is filled with memories of past years, including angels to remind us of those who sang as a heavenly host on the first Christmas and stars to help us remember the one that shone above the stable in Bethlehem.

These and other traditions help our family focus on Christ's birth. Not one of these customs is in the Bible. However, we don't consider these activities blasphemous.

Would a Christmas tree help, hinder, or have no real effect on your celebration of Christ's birth? You and your husband are the only ones who can prayerfully answer this question for your family.

❦ ❦ ❦ ❦ ❦ ❦ ❦

Q How can I get over the guilt I feel when I see how many Christmas presents my sister gives her children and how few things I can afford to give my children?

A Time is a priceless gift that can never be tied with a bow. A parent will never be replaced by the most sophisticated high-tech toy or the Barbie with the most glamorous dress. Children need time with people who love them far more than they need things.

❧ ❧ ❧ ❧ ❧ ❧ ❧

*Q Does getting a child's picture taken with Santa hurt his under-
standing of the real meaning of Christmas?*

A Not necessarily, if your family celebration centers on Jesus'
birthday.
If you feel uncomfortable pretending Santa is "real," you
might choose to tell your child about the historical figure of Saint
Nicholas, the person on whom the contemporary Santa Claus is
based. Hearing about someone who researchers indicate was a
kind man can help a child view Santa as a historical figure.

The key is to emphasize the real meaning of Christmas throughout the holidays. Here are some ways:

• Serve a decorated birthday cake for Jesus as the holiday
dessert.

• Fill a manger for Jesus. Have family members place a piece of
straw in a basket "manger" for each loving action they do during
the holiday season.

• Read bedtime books that focus on the real meaning of
Christmas.

❧ ❧ ❧ ❧ ❧ ❧ ❧

*Q My son complained all through the holidays that "Christmas is for
little kids." How can I prevent him from being disappointed in
future years?*

A Develop family traditions that will grow with your child. For
example, you might drive around to see Christmas lights,
attend a special theater or musical production, participate

in a particular worship service or church activity, or become involved in an annual community-service project. Without focusing attention on your son, show your own enjoyment of these activities.

Also encourage him to view the holidays as a prime time for gathering family history. Encourage him to turn on the tape recorder and ask grandparents about Christmas when they were growing up. He can add to the family tree or gather information to add to the family history each year when relatives come together.

Your son also might enjoy a specific role. For example, he could run the video camera each year to capture highlights of the season or be in charge of organizing the family gift exchange.

But focusing on the real gift of Christmas, the birth of Jesus, is the only aspect of Christmas that will never be disappointing. Support your son as he opens his heart to the Christ Child. Encourage his participation at meaningful holiday worship services. Help him find avenues to show what it means that Jesus is the reason for the season.

🌿 🌿 🌿 🌿 🌿 🌿 🌿

Q *I always dreamed of being a mom, baking Christmas cookies with two little girls. Now I have the two little girls, but the cookies were a disaster and the kitchen was a mess. Whenever I try a project like this, especially at Christmas, it doesn't work. What am I doing wrong?*

A The mental image of Currier and Ives and our selective memories of Christmases past can get all tangled up with reality.

When beginning a mother/daughter project, identify what you want to accomplish. Then ask yourself if the goal is realistic. If the answer is "yes," plan carefully. In the Christmas-cookie situation, decide what is important to you: Measuring ingredients? Using cookie cutters? Decorating? Delivering to neighbors? Then identify which parts of that process match your daughters' developmental levels. (For example, three year olds love to stir a big bowl of dough and decorate about three cookies.) Also, ask your children what they enjoy. A five year old might define making cookies as "shaking on sprinkles," while a ten year old could successfully work through the whole process.

Finally, match the right elements of the project with your children. If the measuring and mixing are important, let the girls help collect the utensils and stir. Then you cut and bake. If decorating counts, use a box mix, and then call the girls when it's time to decorate.

Use a similar approach with any parent/child kitchen or craft project. Even then, not every dream will come true. Just don't let those dashed dreams cloud enjoyable moments with your children.

✺ ✺ ✺ ✺ ✺ ✺ ✺

Q *I dread the week after Christmas and before the kids go back to school. What can make it bearable?*

A Do you want the week to be fun? Purposeful? Be realistic about goals for the week. Then plan ahead. You might want to consider some after-Christmas traditions:

• Visit relatives one family at a time, even if you just saw them. The dynamics are different when the group is smaller.

• View light displays throughout the week.

• Add finishing touches to your Christmas memories. View the video you'll send to far-away relatives, or organize photos shot during the holidays.

• Play or read individually with each child for fifteen minutes a day. Or, set a goal to keep the television set turned off between Christmas and New Year's Day. On January 1, discuss how that affected your family.

• Spend quiet time writing thank-you notes.

• On New Year's Eve, turn the clock forward a few hours (so midnight comes before bedtime) and thank God for the many blessings of the past year.

🐦 🐦 🐦 🐦 🐦 🐦 🐦

Q Do teachers send thank-you letters anymore? My daughter didn't get a note from hers after Christmas, and I remember how much those notes from a teacher meant to me when I was little.

A Yes, as a matter of courtesy and also to model good behavior, teachers do sent thank-you notes. This was probably just an oversight.

Next year, be sure the gift tag is tightly fastened onto the gift. When children pile presents onto a teacher's desk, it's easy for bows and tags to come off. This happened to me several times as a classroom teacher, and I felt bad when I couldn't thank a child and her parent for their thoughtfulness.

🐦 🐦 🐦 🐦 🐦 🐦 🐦

Q If I let my children attend an Easter-egg hunt, will I be supporting a pagan tradition?

A Not necessarily. Many customs that have been adopted by Christians have pagan origins, including the use of eggs at

Easter. According to some sources, even the word *Easter* is pagan: the original meaning was "springtime." Historically, spring rituals in Europe included the giving and coloring of eggs.

Christians expanded on the initial symbolism of the egg, which was simply a sign of new life in spring. Church members painted eggs with Christian symbols and shared decorated eggs with friends as a sign of their common faith in the risen Savior. Even now, around Easter, in some ethnic bakeries you can buy bread with eggs baked whole into bread crust.

Many years ago, these baked eggs were painted red, which some experts interpret as a representation of the blood of Christ. Egg rolling, which can be traced back to the Middle Ages, symbolized the stone rolling away from Christ's tomb.

Today, some families have continued to expand on the Easter egg symbolism. For example, if your children attend that Easter-egg hunt, they might look for the golden egg. If your child finds this "Resurrection egg," he might receive a new Bible or other Christian gift. During the children's sermon on Easter Day, your child might receive an egg with a Christian symbol.

Participation in an Easter-egg hunt is a matter of personal choice. What's important is whether or not this custom, and other traditions that you celebrate, help your child focus on the real meaning of Easter.

🥚 🥚 🥚 🥚 🥚 🥚 🥚

Q I don't like to give my children Easter baskets filled with candy, but it's hard to find other small things that fit into a little basket. What do you suggest?

A Instead of a basket, use a sturdy bucket that can be used all summer at the sandbox or beach. Or, pack goodies in a batting helmet or bike basket. Simply think of a container that your child will need to use at a later time, and purchase that now to use as the Easter "basket."

Instead of candy, try some of these gifts: small construction sets, action figures or vehicles; miniature dolls; comb and brush; barrettes or ponytail holders; bubbles; coins; note pad; fancy markers that change color; colored pencils or chalk; ball; Play-Doh; jump rope; craft supplies; stickers; rubber stamps and stamp pad; mini puzzle. If your children might miss the candy, include some packs of sugarless gum to satisfy the sweet tooth.

❧ ❧ ❧ ❧ ❧ ❧ ❧

Q *At the end of the school year and beginning of summer, there are so many children's activities that I can't go to everything. How can I choose?*

A Ask your children to list all the plays, recitals, programs, games, field trips, and other activities to which parents are invited. Then, ask them to prioritize which are most important for you to attend. Sometimes we assume one activity is more important than another and our children have a totally different perspective, so it's best to make these decisions using input from your children.

❧ ❧ ❧ ❧ ❧ ❧ ❧

Q *Why does my daughter get so whiny at the end of every school year?*

A As the school year winds down, children sense change. Even good change brings uncertainty. Your daughter has been living with a consistent routine for nine months, so any major disruption will include a time of transition followed by new patterns. This can be very unsettling to some children.

Also, your child might be sorry to see the school year end. Some children become very attached to their teachers. Other children know they won't see friends for a couple months. These feelings are totally normal.

Years ago, I read a picture book to my children that included a line I've always remembered: "A little bit sad about the place you are leaving, a little bit happy about the place you are going." That's the way your daughter might feel.

At the end of the school year, when we are going so many directions, it's easy to forget to take time to listen. Allow your daughter many opportunities to talk about her feelings. Being a good listener is one of the best forms of emotional support.

🍎 🍎 🍎 🍎 🍎 🍎 🍎

Q *Instead of imposing on friends to host our family of four on vacation this summer, I want to stay in hotels. But how can I cut costs?*

A Consider these suggestions:
1. Ask a travel agent to find the lowest rates. They often know about special values or will contact hotels directly to locate the best possible rate. Your place of employment might also receive lower business rates that are also available to employees on vacation.

2. Join a frequent traveler club with a single hotel chain. You can earn bonus points for merchandise or travel awards or earn free nights with frequent stays. Club membership is usually free.

3. Look for hotels that offer free cribs, free rollaways, and free

lodging and food for children. Some hotels also have special summer programs with free video-game use or free game packs.

4. Book hotel rooms with a small refrigerator so you can prepare simple meals. This generally saves on food bills.

5. Contact in advance the tourist or convention bureau of cities through which you'll travel. The brochures and booklets often contain information about special rates. When you travel, stop at state welcome centers, which generally provide hotel and attraction coupons.

6. Ask about "family packages" for specific cities or regions, which sometimes offer lodging, food, and attractions at lower rates.

$$\text{🐞 🐞 🐞 🐞 🐞 🐞 🐞}$$

Summer should be the time that kids can just play, but how can my kids do that when all the other kids are in day camp or child-care?

The situation you describe—of childless neighborhoods on summer days—is typical today. The increased number of single-parent and two-income families has resulted in an explosion of organized child care options during the summer.

The pace, activities, and tone of summer reflects the family life and structure of each generation. Look for social opportunities for your children wherever possible: the summer reading program at the library, evening concerts in the park, museum classes, and zoo programs.

❧ ❧ ❧ ❧ ❧ ❧ ❧

Q What is the right age for my daughter to go away to camp for the first time?

A The answer depends on numerous factors. For example: Has the child had positive overnight experiences in the past? Will the child attend with friends? How long will the child be gone? What will the child feel she's missing at home while she's at camp? Are you confident that the camp will offer a safe environment for your child? Also, ask your child a very important question: "Do you want to go?"

These answers will form the basis of your decision. Also, clarify the goals for attending camp and identify other ways those same goals can be met. For example, helping a child gain independence is a goal that often can be met through a camping experience. But that goal can also be achieved by following a grocery list, getting ice from the machine in a hotel, etc.

Adopting a thoughtful approach to this decision will help you match a camp experience to your child's developmental level and clarify your personal goals for her.

❧ ❧ ❧ ❧ ❧ ❧ ❧

Q I liked the county fair when I was young, but when we took our children last year, they acted badly. Are kids today too sophisticated or advanced for these kinds of things?

A No. But before you try again, consider these points:
1. What are your expectations? If you like the quilt and pie exhibits, it might be best to attend alone. Then, on another

day, take the children to areas that will interest them. Discuss, in advance, what your children might like to see and do.

2. Although there are usually many food options, pack along a small, familiar snack or juice in case the food lines are long. Take wet wipes and sunscreen.

3. Locate the bathroom immediately after you arrive.

4. Get a map or overview of what is available. Is there a petting barn? Are clowns doing face painting? Is there a tractor pull or another event that might interest your children? Consider the day's temperature, your children's moods, and your own interests as you mentally plan your time.

5. Remember that although clowns, balloons, and carnival rides can all be fun, the noise and unfamiliar sights can be unsettling to children. Be flexible.

❦ ❦ ❦ ❦ ❦ ❦ ❦

Q *Our Fourth of July family picnic was a disaster. Some marriages had split and my kids' favorite cousins weren't there. How do you know when family traditions should change?*

A You've already stated an important point: family traditions go through life cycles. Traditions can be the glue that holds families together. Family-life researchers consistently show that celebrating traditions is one aspect of healthy families. However, sometimes traditions outlive their value.

Before your next gathering, identify the pluses and minuses of your traditions. Think through the issues now, before you are pressed by time and influenced by the emotional baggage of "we've always done it that way."

As parents, our immediate families represent two generations, so we must take the lead in shaping traditions. We must assume the responsibility to welcome new members, honor our elders, and bridge the past, present, and future for our children.

Does your memory-building Fourth of July picnic fit your family? That's a question only you and other family members can answer.

❧ ❧ ❧ ❧ ❧ ❧ ❧

Q *Do you have any ideas for children's games appropriate for a neighborhood picnic?*

A Check out idea books from the library that feature cross-age and noncompetitive games. Look for activities that the children can do without a lot of supervision while adults socialize. For starters:

• Plan a parade. Encourage children to bring their "wheels": Big Wheels, tricycles, wagons, bikes, etc. Provide streamers, balloons, and crepe paper for decorating. Have a parade through the neighborhood with prizes for the "funniest," "most colorful," and "most imaginative" decorations.

• Have a sidewalk-chalk art show. Provide sidewalk chalk, buckets of water to wet down pavement, and old paint brushes. Children or various groups of people can decorate sections of sidewalk or pavement. The art will disappear with the next rain.

• Sponsor a contest to decorate a watermelon. Tempera paints and brushes, spangles, fabric scraps, glue, and glitter can decorate the exteriors of the soon-to-be dessert.

• Have a two-kilometer walk around the neighborhood to pick up trash. Give each child a bag for litter collection.

• Sponsor a neighborhood garden contest with the kids as the judges.

❧ ❧ ❧ ❧ ❧ ❧ ❧

Q *My kids love vacations, but I almost resent that I do all the driving, the packing, and the unpacking, and they just enjoy. How can I get them to help?*

A Assign regular chores on traveling days, just as you would at home. For example, one child might be responsible for emptying the car trash bag at noon each day; your oldest child might wash the car windshield every time you stop for gas. Also, give each child specific items to carry into the motel. For example, the children might be responsible for their own bags plus one other item. Children should rinse out their swimsuits and hang them up to dry, just as they would at home. Everyone could check around the motel room (especially under beds and in the bathroom) to make sure all items are repacked at the end of your stay.

Look for other opportunities to share responsibilities. That is, after all, part of having a happy family vacation.

❧ ❧ ❧ ❧ ❧ ❧ ❧

Q *How can we avoid a backseat battleground on a long car trip?*

A Plan in advance and be proactive. For example, begin with a physical inspection of your children's seating areas. Are any leftover drinking straws poking up? Any seat belts twisted? Add a trash bag next to each seat. Pack along extra bags, because these will need to be replaced after each day of driving.

If children are out of car seats, set up a seat rotation system. Sitting by the driver and at a window are the desired places. Clip an index card onto the car visor. Then children switch seats at each rest stop according to the chart. This provides a constantly changing environment.

Also, think ahead to the kinds of experiences from which your children can benefit while riding. Designate a special activity for each seat. One seat can be a listening center. Put a cassette player, extra batteries, and tapes at that place. Another seat can be for reading. Another place can be for drawing materials or for sorting baseball cards. At each seat, package appropriate materials in shoe boxes or clear plastic, reusable bags. This advance planning guarantees a comfortable, interesting ride.

Also, pack a cooler with favorite refreshments. Offer drinks about twenty minutes before a planned rest stop. Plan to stop at museums and historic sites, which usually have cleaner bathrooms than gas stations.

Under-pack your car. Children frequently get restless when they are smashed between gear bags and suitcases. They need physical and emotional space between them and their siblings.

🍎 🍎 🍎 🍎 🍎 🍎 🍎

Is there any way to prevent my kids from begging me to buy trashy tourist junk on vacation?

As a family, determine in advance what you will purchase. Consider these possibilities:
• Christmas tree ornaments.
• Refrigerator magnets.
• Rocks from each state for a rock garden.
• Items made from indigenous materials (shell, volcanic ash, local wood, copper, geode, palm leaves, dried cactus).
• Artwork representative of the region you visit.

• One beach towel for each member of the family.

• One T-shirt or sweatshirt for each member of the family. (This makes a nice souvenir and adds to the wardrobe.)

ℑ ℑ ℑ ℑ ℑ ℑ ℑ

Q I can't afford a summer trip this year. How can I make my vacation time seem special for my boys?

A Plan many of the activities you would do on a trip away from home.

For example, mark your vacation dates on the calendar. This will give everyone a visual reminder of a time to anticipate. Also, try to schedule one activity for which you will need tickets. Just the excitement of having tickets in advance makes the time seem special.

Also, think about food. Some of the fun of travel is eating differently. Plan a picnic in the park on one day. Or, drive to a different fast-food restaurant than you'd normally visit.

Gather travel brochures from museums and historical sites in your immediate area.

Ask your boys to suggest places they'd like to visit. Then, when you make some day trips, take along "vacation toys." Check out cassette tapes or books from the library; and use them only when you "travel."

Also, collect memories of your special time together. Borrow a camera from the public library. Add these photos to the ticket stubs, wildflowers you collected and pressed from the picnic, and a brochure from the museum you visited. Arrange the items in a collage and then frame your memories.

$ $ $ $ $ $ $

Q *How much say should kids have in what we do on vacation?*

A Children can make choices within the boundaries you set on time, distance, and cost. Let them share in decision making when possible and appropriate.

Begin with smaller decisions. For example, if you pull off the highway and there's a McDonald's on one side and an Arby's on another, a child might want to choose where to eat lunch.

Only offer a choice when you'd be comfortable with whatever is decided. For example, you might say, "Should we visit the natural history museum that has a dinosaur display or go to the zoo?" One child might choose on one day and another child choose when the next opportunity arises.

Index